How to Survive a Pisces

Real Life Guidance on How to Get on and be Friends with the Last Sign of the Zodiac

First published by O-Books, 2009
O-Books is an imprint of John Hunt Publishing Ltd., Laurel House, Station Approach,
Alresford, Hants, SO24 9JH, UK
office1@o-books.net
www.o-books.com

For distributor details and how to order please visit the 'Ordering' section on our website.

Text copyright: Mary L. English 2008

ISBN: 978 1 84694 252 5

A CIP catalogue record for this book is available from the British Library.

Design: Stuart Davies

Printed in the UK by CPI Antony Rowe
Printed in the USA by Offset Paperback Mfrs, Inc

We operate a distinctive and ethical publishing philosophy in all
areas of our business, from our global network of authors to
production and worldwide distribution.

How to Survive a Pisces

Real Life Guidance on
How to Get on and be Friends
with the Last Sign of the Zodiac

Mary L English

BOOKS

Winchester, UK
Washington, USA

CONTENTS

Also by Mary L English

The Birth Charts of Indigo Children
6 Easy Steps in Astrology

Please visit Mary L English's site at www.maryenglish.co.uk

This book is dedicated to my soul-mate, partner, husband lover and ally: Jonathan who has waited patiently, as all good Taureans do, for 2 years for me to complete this book, so that he will truly know 'How To Survive A Pisces'.

Acknowledgements

I would like to thank the following people:

Dr Stephen Gascoigne for being the Pisces that recognised how to heal those parts of me I'd forgotten about.

Nicky Webb for being the Pisces that has such faith in my ideas.

Marina a lovely Pisces who helped me in the beginning.

Mel for being the Pisces that brought healing to my family.

My son for being the Libran that makes me always look on the other side.

My mother Jean English for being the Aquarius who was excited that I was writing a book.

My older sister Lucy for being the Aquarius who knows that our books are our babies.

Filey and Fynn for having faith in me.

Mabel, Jessica and Usha for their understanding.

Laura and Mandy for their friendship.

Donna Cunningham for her help and advice

Alois Treindl for being the Pisces that founded the wonderful Astro.com website

Judy Ramsell Howard at the Bach Centre for her encouragement

John my publisher for being the person that fought tooth and nail to get this book published and all the staff at O-Books including Andy, Stuart and Trevor.

And last but not least my lovely clients for their valued contributions.

Introduction

Why the title? I have been interested in divination and mystical things since my early teens, when Neptune started working its way through my 4th House of Home and Family. First of all I read cards for friends and family. My first reading was for a friend on holiday. My Mum had bought a book on Card Reading using playing cards and my friend and I laid out the cards and did a spread. I read out the meanings for each of the cards in the spread and I was amazed at the accuracy of what was there. My friend was too.

I then taught myself to read palms and read all of Cheiro's works. What a great palmist he was, and what a grand ego! I also read Linda Goodman's Sun Signs[17] and found it easy to understand the characters she wrote about. I didn't see myself as the fluffy Pisces she described but some of it seemed to fit.

When I was 18 I joined The Society for the Study of Physiological Patterns and went to meetings in London. I had no idea how to make a living out of what I'd learned and after a few months of doing readings in my small bed-sit in Harrow, with not enough money to feed the meter, I gave up and went into retailing.

I still 'read' for my close friends and kept a trusty pack of playing cards especially for that purpose.

Years later after my son was born I decided to become a Homeopath when I home-treated him for croup, with great success.

Then when my Homeopath remarked to me in a consultation about some event that had happened and it 'must have been' during my 'Saturn Return' and I asked her what that meant, and she said 'never mind', I was off. She knew about something that I didn't. So I came home and read as much as I could on the subject and taught myself Astrology. The hard way, the reading-every-book-I-could-lay-my-hands-on, making-up hundreds of charts and talking them through with my best friend, looking at my own chart and finding out that even though I was a floppy Pisces, I had a nice firm Leo Ascendant to keep me in check and protect me from the worst parts of being the last sign of The Zodiac.

Two of my sisters have an understanding of Astrology and my Aunt used to draw up charts, even though she was a Catholic but what stopped me from deeply learning Astrology was the maths involved. Have you ever seen an old book on how to draw up a chart? Do you know how long it takes? So it wasn't until the advent of computer programmes that Astrology became available to me in a form I could easily access.

When my lovely Aunt died, I asked my Uncle if I could have her Astrology books and he gave me her Astrological 'Bible' : The New Waite's Compendium of Natal Astrology with Ephemeris for 1880-1980 and Universal Table of Houses. She had faithfully recorded all my family's dates of birth, their times (thank you Auntie Jo!), and various other friends and acquaintances. Even the Pope and people in the news, so I had plenty of information to work on there. But it wasn't until 1996, when Neptune and Uranus started to transit my 6th house of Work that I finally decided to become a professional Astrologer , as opposed to a part-time closet one. Uranus allowed me to come out of my shell. I also joined the Astrological Association who were very helpful and encouraging.

I finished my Homeopathy training in 2001 and my Homeopathy practice was doing very well. Then the manager of a mystical shop in our town centre asked me if I'd come and work there, as there aren't very many palmists around. I developed a practice that included palmistry, Astrology and card readings. Buy one get 2 free..

I also took a short course in counselling skills at my local college which helped me considerably to be empathic and aware of my clients' needs.

It was at this time that I started to come across more Pisces than I'd ever met in my whole life. Pisces live and breathe the world of the mystical, the weird, the wonderful and they spend an awful lot of money on readings as they don't trust people in authority. They'd rather have someone skilled in esoteria guiding them, than a bank manager or police person. And even if the clients I met weren't Pisces, if they were in a tangled relationship, or their lives were in a dreadful mess, always, underneath it all, would be a Pisces, who was not *causing* all the difficulties.

Pisces don't *cause* things, they just happen to be there when weird things happen!

So I thought, as an enlightened Pisces, who had decided to mend my Pisces ways, that it would be a good idea to tell my suffering clients, and those further afield, how to make the best of the Pisces in their lives, so they don't enter the dreadful, messy, tangled, wobbly messes that Pisces can so easily lead themselves and others. So this isn't a self-help book. It's not aimed at Pisces themselves (although they might learn a lot about themselves by reading it) it was written for others to help their Pisces child or understand their Pisces lover, or get the best from their Pisces employee, boss or sister-in-law.

So where to start? Tell you not to date, marry, employ, love a Pisces?

No, of course not. But at least go into the ring with your eyes, ears and 6th sense *very* open.

To understand a star sign, it helps if you understand a little about Astrology. We all read our horoscopes in the papers. Who hasn't, when they've had a bad day, wanted to have a sneaky read of what their sign is up to at the moment? Taurus likes to hear they are going to have a cash windfall, Aquarius likes to read that 'new' things are going to happen in their lives and equally Capricorn likes to find out that their hunches were correct and it will be a bad year and they'd better batten-down the hatches.

But what happens if those little words of wisdom don't really rock your boat? What happens if you're a nice peaceful Aries who is calm and collected or a Gemini too shy to speak? What happens when the 'profile' that has been attributed to your sign, just doesn't compute? That's because all you are looking at is the Sun sign, not the complete picture.

Each of us has our own unique Birth Chart. Each of us was born at a different time and in a different place to most of the people in our lives. I once made the chart of two identical twins and they were completely different characters because one had a Pisces Ascendant and the other had an Aquarius Ascendant............but before we plunge deep into all the jargon, let me make one thing perfectly crystal clear.

Unless you were born at exactly the same date, time and location as someone else, your chart will be different. You will be different, and it is those differences we are going to learn about.

So to survive your Pisces, you need to identify your Pisces and I will make it as clear and as easy as I can for you to do that, but first we need to learn a little about Astrology and how it came about in the first place and where is today.

"Astrology is the science that explores the action of celestial bodies upon animate and inanimate objects, and their reactions to such influences."

Astrology dates back to early human civilization and is the parent of astronomy; for many years they were one science. Modern astrology has its source in what was called Sumer and is now known as Iraq.

'The people there, who called their land Sumer, quite suddenly and inexplicably began to build large, walled cities out of sun-dried mud bricks on the banks of the two great rivers (Tigris and Euphrates) and dug an extensive network of irrigation canals that allowed them to grow, in the fertile soil, an abundance of wheat, barley, millet and sesame, whose surplus they traded with their neighbors for the wood, metal and stone that the region lacked. In time, the growing wealth of the cities led to the formation of a non-productive priestly class, who had both the opportunity and the incentive to study the stars. These men were the first astrologers.'[1]

The priests of this kingdom made the discovery which developed into what we now call astronomy and the zodiacal system of the planets which we call astrology today.

For many generations they painstakingly recorded the movements of these heavenly bodies. Eventually, they discovered, by careful calculation that in addition to the Sun and the Moon, five other visible planets moved in specific directions every day. These were the planets that we now call Mercury, Venus, Mars, Jupiter and Saturn. The priests lived highly secluded lives in monasteries adjacent to massive pyramidal observation towers called ziggurats. Every day they observed the movements of the planets and noted down any corresponding earthly phenomena from floods to rebellions.

They came to the conclusion that the laws which governed the movements of the stars and planets also governed events on Earth.

In the beginning the stars and planets were regarded as being actual gods. Later, as religion became more sophisticated, the two ideas were separated and the belief developed that the god 'ruled' the corresponding planet.

Gradually, a highly complex system was built up in which each planet had a particular set of properties ascribed to it. This system was developed partly through the reports of the priests and partly though the natural characteristics of the planets. Mars was seen to be red in colour and was therefore identified with the god Nergal, the fiery god of war and destruction.

Venus, identified by the Sumerians as their goddess Inanna was the most prominent in the morning, giving birth as it were, to the day. She therefore became the planet associated with the female qualities of love and gentleness, as well as with the function of procreation. The observation of the stars by the Sumerians was mostly a religious act. The planets were their gods and each visible object was associated with an invisible spiritual being that judged their actions, blessed them with good fortune or sent them tribulations. A slight case of projection, but none-the less the planets helped the Sumerians develop some meaning and sense to their lives as they had got the hang of farming and land management, and the more mundane aspects of life. They now wanted to explore their spiritual selves. Astrology and the study of the planets allowed them to do this.

The Sumerian priests made associations between earthly events like floods and famine with a particular phase of the Moon, by seeing an evening 'star' or by the appearance of a comet. After a time they then noted that the heavenly bodies had various cycles and it became possible for them to mathematically determine when, for instance, the Moon might be eclipsed, so they could then forecast certain events. This information was reserved only for the king and not distributed on a mass scale as it is today.

Astrology didn't happen over night. It began with observation, something that is somewhat lost in the modern world. We don't have the time today to watch, wait, and observe. We read about something, see it on the telly, go out and buy it and expect 'bingo' for our problems to cease. Time for contemplation and observation is reserved for the Tibetan monks or the clinically depressed.

In medieval times Astrologers were also Astronomers. They knew where the stars and the planets were, plus they were educated and could read and write. With the advent of schools and computers, we can now enjoy the fruits of these people's hard work by turning a page or clicking a mouse, but nothing will replace observing how people are and how they interact with each other.

There are two types of Astrology practiced in the west. Tropical Astrology which gives the position of a planet by sign and Sidereal which gives the position by constellation. Over 4,000 years ago, on the vernal equinox, the first day of Spring, the Sun was in the constellation of Aries. Now because of the Earth wobbling on its axis and a thing called 'precession', the Sun enters in the sign of Aries but in the constellation of Pisces. I practice Tropical Astrology, taking into account that as far as the planets are today, they've shifted. Both systems have value, there is no 'right' or 'wrong' I just prefer the older one.

So let us learn about the sign we are going to survive.

Mary L English, Bath 2008

Chapter One

The Sign

"The crux of Pisces is the fishes swimming in opposite directions. I interpret this as the gravitational pull of the material world against aspirations for the spiritual. I think this is central to how I experience my existence." Male Pisces.

"I find being a Pisces a bit of a rollercoaster sometimes! I can talk myself right in and right out of any decision, any subject, any time!! Having said that I will finally jump on pure gut instinct and get a good result - but usually far different to my initial intentions!! Pisces troubles usually happen if you ignore the inner voice and go with a rational choice...there is nothing rational about us and we usually end up telling ourselves off for not trusting! My advice to a partner is to stand back and watch with amusement while all the debating goes on inwardly and just wait for the final decision!" Female Pisces.

"I have been out with one and my brother is one. I find Pisces sensitive, creative and sometimes psychic. The Pisces lady I went out with was extremely sensitive and a romantic, very caring. I (please don't be offended) have found Pisces don't always know what direction they are heading in, almost like lost souls. My uncle who is Pisces and my brother are incredibly caring and loving towards their children. I find on the whole they are giving people but are often classed as being wishy washy." Female Gay Aquarius talking about Pisces.

The Sign of Pisces
So, what or who is a Pisces?

First of all they have to be born when the Sun is in Pisces. This is an Astrological term for the movement of the planets through the signs. Each sign changes every month and it can change sign at any time of the day or night. The average dates for your Pisces is February the 20th to March 20th.

If your Pisces was born at 2am on February 20th 1988 they'd be a Pisces Sun sign. However if they were born at 11.50pm on 20th March 1988 they'd be an Aries because at approx 9pm on the evening of the 20th March, the Sun then moved into the next sign of the Zodiac, which is Aries.

I have come across quite a few people who were born on the 20th of the month who thought they were one sign and found out they'd thought all their life they were that sign, when in fact they were the next sign on. So *be sure* you check your Pisces' birth date with an Astrologer or a good computer programme before you decide that you have a Pisces in your life.

Mind you, it would be a bit difficult to confuse a Pisces with an Aries, they are such different personalities, but when you take all the other characteristics of a chart into account, you might occasionally get an Aries who is gentle, quiet, dreamy and sensitive. Not often,but occasionally..

Sometimes there are Pisces who don't follow astrology. Patrick Moore the Astronomer is one. A Pisces who denies the existence of Astrology?!!...........Ahh, but he understands the stars and all things celestial plus he's got a Gemini Ascendant and Sun conjunct Uranus. It's too late for him now (he's in his late 80's) to learn Astrology but I'm sure if he did, he'd glean the same satisfaction that Astrologers get from their craft.

In fact, in the old days, Astronomers were Astrologers, the two things operated hand-in-hand. To be an Astronomer and to study the stars, meant you needed to be educated. It also meant you had to have an understanding of mathematics as plotting the paths of the planets and stars involved complicated number crunching. Luckily, for me, the advent of computers has taken that task away. We can now plot the path of a planet through a sign by clicking a mouse. Some poor bod had to make those calculations originally and write the programme. But just like re-inventing the wheel, the computer has prevented us from having to start from scratch and allowed us to get stuck-in with the interpretation of a chart and spend less time on the calculation.

So who or what is a Pisces?

Well, they are a group of people born (as we have discovered) between Feb 20th and March the 20th. So how can we lump them all together and decide they have the same characteristics? By observation. Astrology is about 'as above, so below'. That the planets reflect aspects of who we are. It's a romantic view. I'm sure there isn't much science can do to explain it. Maybe its more about the phenomena of groups of people but it was decided, a long, long time ago that Pisces was a constellation in the sky and that in some way reflected an amount of people on our planet and the way they conducted their daily lives.

Astrologers over the centuries have made observations, explained, deduced, calculated all for one purpose. To help us understand our lives, our motivations and realise our desires. The conclusions an Astrologer will draw-up about your chart are from a mass body of thought that has built up over the years.

I must at this point add a codicil. Even though everything you read in this book, may or may not make any sense to you, please don't make any major decisions about your life because of it. There are hundreds of trained counsellors, advisors, astrologers, homeopaths and alternative therapists who can help you make the changes in your life that you need.

That's not to say that your Astrological journey won't be interesting. It will but I have seen and heard of people selling their houses, or relocating or changing their jobs, because they were 'told' by a fortune teller or astrologer that this would be the case. I rarely give this type of advice because I might be putting ideas into people heads that shouldn't be there. If you weren't even considering moving house, or relocating, making a major life change just from a 1 hour 'reading' from someone you hardly know, to me, isn't a great idea. By all means listen to the advice that has been given but please chat it over with your friends and family first. And sleep on it.

Which brings me to one aspect of Pisces that is never a problem. Being able to sleep. I don't think I've ever treated a Pisces for sleeplessness. I can sleep anywhere. On a bus on a train, in a car on an airplane. I'm sure I could have a little kip for a few mins standing up if I let myself.

"But Pisceans are in some ways their own worst enemies. Their imaginations tend to run away with them, particularly in conflict situations. They need to have trust in the people around them. Pisceans need lots of sleep, and not to intellectualise too much!"

How true!

Here we have a Pisces summing-up their own short-comings. They have good imaginations, they don't enjoy conflict and being too intellectual for too long will wear them out. Pisces sort of float in and out of situations. They're like the gossamer on spider's webs, the fog or mist that you find at dawn. The mistiness you get in your eyes when you're just about to cry. Pisces are from this world but they're not truly in it.

There is even a Pisces Astrologer called Linda Reid who wrote a book about the astrology of dreaming called 'Crossing the Threshold'[5]. She makes a chart for the time you had the dream, records the dream, discusses it with you and counsels you to make valuable life changes. Only a Pisces could do that. Develop a form of counseling that involves making a birth chart for the time you had the dream, and uses that chart to guide her clients to wholeness. Super!

As long as you can understand how a Pisces works, then your expectations will be in-line with what they can deliver. Don't ask a double Pisces to run a marathon or work in an abattoir. I'm sure they can do these things, but they won't do them in earnest or enjoy them.

Just the same as any other sign, a Pisces can do a job that is boring or repetitive, or soul-less, but they'll be working against the grain. This book is about how to get the best from your Pisces and enhance yours and their lives.

The best definition of a Pisces that I have found is by Felix Lyle in The Instant Astrologer[9] and includes the keywords: sensitive, receptive, compassionate, imaginative, self-sacrificing, impressionable, passive, escapist, acquiescent, confused and over-emotional.

All of these qualities will be evident as we go further into discovering the Pisces in your life and we will be discussing how to cope with those attributes, how to understand them and how to make the best use of those character traits.

To get the best from the Pisces in your life, you need to understand a few things about astrology and how things work. I shall take you through enough information in a birth chart to help you make the right decisions, make the most helpful choices and (hopefully) learn a little about what motivates a Pisces and how they view the world. Because I can guarantee they see things far differently from you. For instance, say you were a Gemini and you went to a rock concert with a Pisces, and there you are talking about the band and the music and the particular tracks you'd enjoyed and how tired you now felt but you were really glad you went and, bye-the-way you bumped into Steve at the drinks stall and he said.....................and your Pisces lover/partner/friend/child/mother or whatever, would be looking at you in a dreamy way, and would reply with the fact that she liked the blue lights on the stage and the song about the broken hearts......and (as she is a water sign) how she now felt exhausted being with all those people and she saw someone who had a moonstone crystal necklace that was *just the same* as hers but it was a bit bluer.................and you think ' did we go to the same concert/gig here?'. 'Were we in the same building?'.................. 'Were we watching the same songs being performed?'........when in reality, you were actually on different wave-lengths, maybe even different planets.

So what planet does Pisces come from because it sure doesn't contain logic or rational thought or planning?

Neptune

"Ye elves of hills, brooks, standing lakes, and groves, And ye that on the sands with printless foot do chase the ebbing Neptune, and do fly him."
Shakespeare

Planet: A celestial body that orbits around the Sun.

Star: With the exception of the Moon and the planets, every fixed point of light in the sky is a star, including the Sun. However in Astrology we use the term 'planet' for all the bits we use. So if you catch me calling the Sun, a planet, that is an Astrological term, not one used in astronomy.

All the star signs, from Aries to Pisces have a 'Planet' that looks after them. We use the term 'rules' them. You could say in a way, that they 'come' from this planet because the planet describes the motivating forces of the sign. The rulerships were decided after years of argument and discussion amongst various astrologers (and is still in dispute each time a new planet is discovered). How to make a chart is covered later, first we will look at the planet that has now been decided 'looks after' Pisces the sign of the fishes.

An understanding of Neptune as a planet and its attributes will help you make more sense of understanding Pisces.

Neptune was nearly discovered by Galileo who first saw it while he was observing the Jupiter system on 28 December 1612. After the discovery of Uranus in 1781 by William Hershel in Bath, UK (where I live) astronomers continued to observe the night sky and track the movements of other celestial bodies. However, Neptune's discovery wasn't made by observation. The astronomers who were working on the case used 'mathematical astronomy'. Uranus wasn't moving as predictions said it would, so the astronomers concluded that another planet must have been affecting its orbit.

Neptune was recorded several more times, without being recognized as a planet, over the following years. Lalande a French astronomer, recorded Neptune on the 8th and 10th of May 1795 thinking that it was a star. William Herschel's son John Herschel, who was involved with the discovery, recorded Neptune on 14 July 1830 also believing it to be a star.

However, a French chap named Urbain Le Verrier, who worked at the Paris Observatory, used mathematical calculation to prove its existence and ... *"discovered a star with the tip of his pen, without any instruments other than the strength of his calculations alone."*He received many honors and widespread recognition for his achievement. The Times carried the headline on the 1 October 1846: *"Le Verrier's planet found"*.George Airy and John Couch Adams were the two other astronomers, who independently worked on 'finding' the planet.

In the aftermath of the discovery, there was much national-istic rivalry between the French and the British over who had priority for the discovery and eventually, after considerable argument, it was decided to give the credit to both Urbain Le Verrier and Adams together.Their discovery was called Neptune.So Neptune the planet was 'found' not by observation, as most of the other planets were discovered, but by mathematical means i.e. Urbain Le Verrier sat there, working out the movements of Uranus, which he (and John Couch Adams) deduced must be influenced by the orbit of another planet, because it was not moving as they thought it would. Neptune was 'in the background', minding its own business, just like Pisces can do, but affecting others (in this case the orbit of Uranus). How quaint! How like a Pisces.................then BAM!! It gets discovered and all hell breaks loose.

Now you might be asking, what has the fact that the planet was called Neptune got to do with how it affects Pisces' lives?

Well, by, what I have said already, the observation of modern Astrologers on how the planet affects the various signs and also the characteristics of its orbit, its movement, what happened historically when the planet was discovered have all been taken into account.

Margaret E Hone wrote in 1951 in her 'Modern Text Book of Astrology'[10] more than 100 years after Neptune was discovered : *"This planet has to do with what hides itself from view, hence it is the most difficult for which to find a suitable one-word description"*.

She then goes on to use the words 'nebulousness, impressionability, artistic, dreamy, emotional, idealistic, imaginative, sensitive, subtle, sentimental, woolly, wandering and unstable' amongst others to convey the sort of themes that Neptune governs.

Plenty has been written about Neptune in myth. The Romans called him the God of the sea, (the Greeks called him Poseidon) and he was Zeus' younger brother. He carried a trident which had three prongs, as is seen it its glyph that Astrologers now use.

In Roman legend, he was given the sea as his realm and he took over the Greek God Poseidon's job of getting into tempestuous rages. His wife, Amphitrite, gave birth to a son called Triton. He was also famed for having love affairs and was the father to several other children who were wild and cruel. He was worshipped as the god of navigation and temples were erected in his honor. Both the Greeks and later the Romans felt this God controlled the seas and when angry would cause storms and shipwrecks. Not a particularly friendly chap and prone to rubbing-up the other Gods in the wrong way.

So having a boss, or ruler as incomprehensible as Neptune, who can so easily take you to the heights of spirituality and just as swiftly take you to the depths of oblivion, you can see that Pisces, the dual fishes, swimming in opposite directions, has a certain amount of Karma to work through before they can be at peace with themselves, or anyone else for that matter.

Water
Female Aries talking about her male Pisces Partner

"I live with a Piscean male and find that "water problems" seem to follow him round. When we first moved in together the house we were renting had just been fully renovated to a high standard yet we managed to have two leaks in the kitchen in the 6 months we stayed there. The home we live in now, we had been living there for about 3 months when water started dripping through the ceiling. In the following months we developed a leak under the sink, a leaking shower (which was replaced), leak from a central heating drain off pipe, leaking gutter x 2, then last week our new shower started to leak (it had only been in 6 months) and within days our central heating boiler was leaking. Finally I feel I must mention that my partner is a twin and his sister's shower also began to leak at the same time ours did in the first instance, and then BOTH our new showers developed the same leak fault within days of each other for the second time AGAIN! Very bizarre! (Thank goodness we know an excellent plumber - we are his best customer ha ha!)

He also has problems with water at his complementary health clinic i.e. hot/cold water machine - would never work correctly, two bubbles lamps (the ones that are like tubes and a pump blows bubbles/changes colors) both lamps broke within days and the water would not flow in them. He also has a couple of water fountains which have also ceased to work......"

To understand Pisces, you also need to get an understanding of water because Pisces has been 'chosen' by Astrologers to be classified under the Element of Water. (see page 24 for Elements)

Now water, as you know, has no structure. It takes the shape of wherever it's placed, so it's just as functional in a beer glass as it is in a water fall. It is still water, no matter where it is and a Pisces will do the same. Meld and melt and form itself around whoever, or wherever it is surrounded by. Water can flow, rush, dribble, drip it has the most amazing properties. Look at the book by Masaru Emoto 'The Hidden Messages in Water'[11] and you'll see how water, which is important to us as humans, and all the animals in the world, can be constructive or destructive. We *need* water, but we have to learn its capabilities and even now, we don't really understand its energies.

What about Homeopathy and the dilution of remedies? Jacques Benveniste conducted experiments on the memory of water but everyone poo pooed the results and guess what star sign this man was? A Pisces. And his mistake? He had a Leo Ascendant and Sun in the 8th house , so he came out of his corner fighting, convinced he was on a mission and everyone else should leave him alone. But they didn't and he paid the price.

As Pisces is a water sign and fishes live in water, we need to understand the qualities of what we are dealing with, because just as water is an everyday element, it also has characteristics we can't easily explain and this is where Pisces hits problems.

They have problems with themselves, knowing who they are, where they're going (the biggest and most asked question from Pisces to me). How can you know where you're going when your tail is tied to another fish who is swimming down stream and you want to go upstream?

With difficulty. With BIG difficulty.

Now, it's pointless saying to a Pisces that's in a puddly mess: "Pull yourself together!". "How?" thinks the Pisces. "I don't know who I **am** to be able to pull that together"..........you get my drift. So Astrology is incredibly useful to describe a Pisces to themselves. It's a very good starting point. And all you really need to know about your Pisces is their Ascendant, their Moon and where their Sun is in their chart.

You can find a lot of other interesting information about your Pisces by having a professional Astrologer draw-up their chart and taking you through what is 'promises'. For a Birth chart is only a promise. It shows potential. Two people with similar charts might have quite different lives if one lives in a hut in the jungle and the other is born into the Royal Family (point of note, not many members of the aristocracy are Pisces and most of them have Leo in their chart.)

For example. I have a Leo Ascendant, so I need to be the centre of attention, not all the time, but in my world and my Moon is in Gemini, making me enjoy conversation and company and verbalising my emotions (or as I do, recording them in my journal) and my Sun is located in the 7th House of Marriage. So I'm happiest being married, chatting and glowing.........

So what are the combinations that you need to know to understand the Pisces in your life? First let's learn how to make a chart and understand enough to get the information we need. You could of course, make an appointment to see an Astrologer, but this is a do- it- yourself book, so I shall show you how to do this from the comfort of your own home.

It does involve using the Internet, so if you're not on-line yet, pop down to your local library and use their computers. It's easier than you think.

Chapter Two

How to make a chart

Using Astrology is like building-up a painting. You start with the outline (the chart) and add some buildings or people (the planets) with a smattering of landscape (the houses) some perspective and then colour. Only when you see all of it together can you make a judgement. And what seems nice to one person, will be horrible to someone else. The same is with Astrologers. Some (me) like the Equal House system, because all the houses are the same size and uniform. Others prefer the Placidus system because they like the fact that the Midheaven is at the 12 o'clock position and makes more 'sense'. I don't do sense that often, I'm a Pisces myself don't forget! But basically, the planets and their position in the sky at the moment of your birth are translated into a circle with 12 segments. Each one of the segments represents a different area of life and each planet can be in any one of the 12 signs from Aries to Pisces.

Are you still with me?

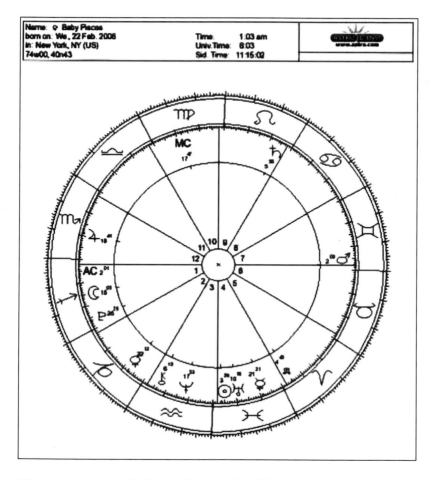

Name: ♀ Baby Pisces
born on: We, 22 Feb. 2006
In: New York, NY (US)
74w00, 40n43
Time: 1:03 am
Univ.Time: 6:03
Sid. Time: 11:16:02

Here is the chart of a little Pisces baby. The chart is the circle with the symbols in. For our purposes, all we need to concentrate on are, what signs and places 3 things are to get a basic understanding of this person.

Here's a quick synopsis of this particular child's chart.

Her **Ascendant** is in the sign of **Sagittarius**, her **Sun** is in the **4th** house and her **Moon** is in the Sign of **Sagittarius** too. So we have some-one who loves to travel, who asks questions, isn't that modest, has a fiery nature but also loves her home and her Mum and is a Pisces, so will love fairy stories and being free to daydream.

The next part in our journey of learning how to get the best out of your Pisces will probably only benefit Mums and Dads of the now as most people I meet of my age only have a vague idea of when they were born (unless they had an Astrologer for an Auntie like me!) so their charts can never be 100% accurate. If you don't know your Pisces birth-time, then just use a default time of 6am. You won't however be able to make an accurate chart, and the houses might be in the wrong order. So only read the info for Sun and Moon, ignore the house information. For this to 'work' you do need an accurate time of birth.

To make your Pisces chart, go to http://www.astro.com and make an account then go to the free horoscopes section and scroll down and use the special part of their site, the 'extended chart section.'

You've already inputted all your data, now *make sure you change the box to say equal-house.* The default system is Placidus and all the houses will be different sizes and for a beginner that's just too confusing.

Your chosen chart will look something like this.

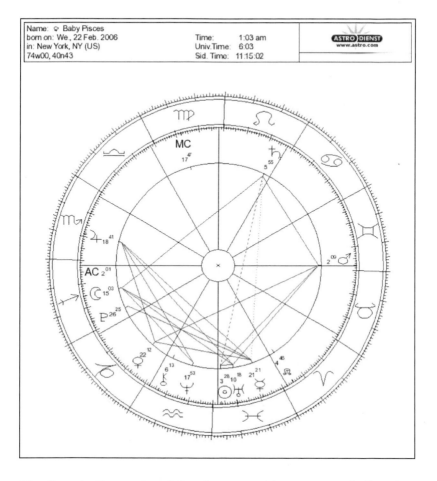

Name: ♀ Baby Pisces
born on: We., 22 Feb. 2006
in: New York, NY (US)
74w00, 40n43

Time: 1:03 am
Univ.Time: 6:03
Sid. Time: 11:15:02

ASTRO)DIENST
www.astro.com

The lines in the centre of the chart are either easy or challenging mathematical associations between each planet in the chart, so ignore them too.

We only want 3 pieces of information. The **sign** of the **Ascendant**, the **sign** the **Moon** is in and the **house** the **Sun** is in.

This is the abbreviation for the Ascendant:

AC

This is the symbol for the Sun: ☉

This is the symbol for the Moon: ☽

The houses are numbered 1-12 in an anti-clockwise order.

The Elements
To understand your Pisces fully, you must take into account which Element their Ascendant and Moon are in.

Each sign of the Zodiac has been given an element that it operates under : Earth, Air, Fire and Water. I like to think of them as operating at different 'speeds'.

The **Earth** signs are **Taurus**, **Virgo** and **Capricorn**. The Earth Element is stable, grounded and concerned with practical matters. Pisces with a lot of Earth in their chart work best at a very slow, steady speed. (I refer to these in the text as 'Earthy')

The **Air** signs are **Gemini**, **Libra** and **Aquarius** (who is the 'Water-carrier' *not* a water sign). The Air element enjoys ideas, concepts and thoughts. It operates at a faster speed than Earth, not as fast as Fire but faster than water and earth. Imagine them as being medium speed.

The **Fire** signs are **Aries**, **Leo** and **Sagittarius**. The Fire element likes action, excitement and can be very impatient. Their speed is *very* fast. (I refer to these as Firey i.e. Fire-Sign)

The **Water** signs are **Cancer**, **Scorpio** and our good friend **Pisces**. The Water element involves feelings, impressions, hunches and intuition. They operate faster than Earth but not as fast as Air. A sort of slow-medium speed.

Chapter Three

The Ascendant

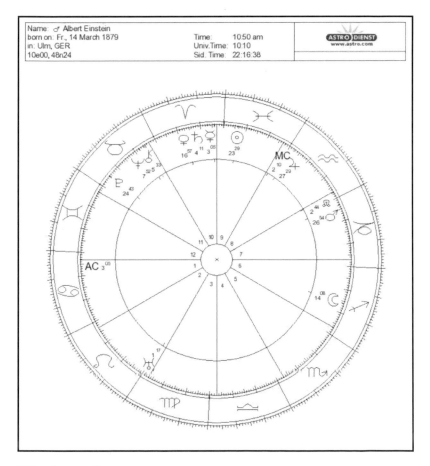

The Ascendant

This is Albert Einstein's chart. Bet you didn't know he was a Pisces! It always makes me smile when I hear some scientist spouting off about how analytical and accurate science is and then they quote Einstein. The man was a Pisces, genius Yes, away-with-the-fairies Yes, scientist Yes but he also had lots of 'faith' and belief which science seems to have now lost. Sad.

The line at the quarter to nine position on the chart says AC 3 05 and is next to the symbol for Cancer which is all you need to know for the moment.

So, Albert had an **Ascendant** in **Cancer**.

The Ascendant is determined by the actual time of birth, so you really need to know the accurate time of birth to get the correct Ascendant because it changes sign every two hours. So someone born at 10am will have a different Ascendant from someone born at 12pm. In astrology we classify the Ascendant as being the outside part of you, the bit people meet first. The image we want people to see in fact the image people *will* see. Your Ascendant is what you display at a party, or to your parents, or when you're under pressure. It's the coat you wear, the glasses you see the world through, how you viewed the world when you came into it. Your beginning.

As you were being born, the Sun was in one sign, the Moon and all the planets were in other signs and *the* most important part of your chart was in a sign signifying how you 'came into the world'. It could be in the sign of Virgo making your Pisces discriminating, analytical and prone to wanting to categorise things. The Earth sign slows the energies down and makes the person more likely to take things at a slower pace than say someone with a Firey Aries Asc who will rush-in-where-angels-fear-to-tred.Or it could have been in the sign of Cancer, wanting to 'feel at home' , loving Mum, wanting protection and financial security.

So someone who has a Fire Sign Ascendant will be more proactive, more of a 'doing' sort than someone with a water Ascendant, who will want to wait, be slower, feel their way into a situation. Understanding the Ascendant explains your Pisces' first breath, how they first saw the world as a baby and it's an important part of a chart. But what if your Pisces is adopted, or their parents have died, or they were born during a black-out or a power cut? Then you have to remember that it will be difficult, not impossible, to make a correct chart. If you know the date, then that at least is a starting point, but for the purposes of this book, you need date, time, location.

So go onto the Internet and get your Pisces' Birthchart and look for the Ascendant. On the circle its at the ¼ to 9 position. It might say ASC on it or AS. That's the Ascendant. It will have a sign there.

These are the shapes representing the signs, so find the one that matches yours. They are called glyphs.

Aries ♈
Taurus ♉
Gemini ♊
Cancer ♋
Leo ♌
Virgo ♍
Libra ♎
Scorpio ♏
Sagittarius ♐
Capricorn ♑
Aquarius ♒
Pisces ♓

Now that you know the Asc you can see how your Pisces views life, or even more importantly, how others see him/her. They can't 'see' the Sun sign, because its hidden behind this mask, and it's important you understand how it works and how it feels. A Libra Ascendant feels very different from a Capricorn Ascendant.

So here are how the various Ascendants combine with a Pisces Sun:

The Ascendant with a Pisces Sun
Aries Ascendant
Aries is a Fire Sign, the first sign of the Zodiac, and as such, needs to feel 'first'. They are likened to the baby that wants attention, so a Pisces with Aries Ascendant will always want to lead, to be first in the queue, they won't want to wait for anyone or anything and might be a bit impatient (all the Fire Signs are).

Taurus Ascendant
Taurus is an Earth sign, and will give a Pisces a more grounded approach. This is actually a more useful Asc for Pisces as being grounded is something they have problems with. They spend so much time being away with the fairies, having this Asc means they'll remember to have lunch, remember to look after their bodies and be happy with a more simple life.However, their finances can be an issue and they might fret about their bank balance.

Gemini Ascendant
Gemini is an Air sign and involves communication and change, and a Pisces with this Asc might move house a lot, be on the phone 24/7, love change and conversation and be capable of communicating with anyone, anywhere. They're good at asking questions, not so good at waiting for an answer...

Cancer Ascendant
Cancer is a Water sign. The sign of the home and family and this is a nice sign for a Pisces to have as it's also a Water sign. Provided this combination has been mothered and cared for in a gentle way when young, they can grow to be quite confident individuals, but sensitivity is the key word here, and a Cancer Asc will make a Pisces more sensitive to disruption and emotional dischord.

Leo Ascendant

Leo is another Fire sign and adds regality and a nice strong exterior for a Pisces. They expect the red carpet to be rolled out for them and like their egos to be stroked, but underneath the Pisces sun will temper the 'please treat me with respect' approach. They're good in a crisis, as the Fire Element will send them in bravely where other signs might fear to tred.

Virgo Ascendant

"I find it hard to be organized and structured, to make decisions and create goals in my life or to feel that I deserve much."

Virgo is an Earth sign and brings a practical approach to life. Virgo Asc is the opposite of the Pisces Sun (as they are opposite signs) so this Pisces combination will want to be able to analyse things, explain things,have reasons for "Life the Universe and Everything." They can also fret more than normal about their health. They need things to be 'ordered' and 'organised'.

Libra Ascendant

Libra is an Air sign and as represented by the scales needs to feel balanced. With this combination, a Pisces will put a lot of energy into their personal love life , their partners and close relationships. Libra Asc also *hates* arguments and people falling out so will do anything to avoid clashes. They like to be surrounded by pleasing decorations, pastel colours, anything as long as it is beautiful as Libra is 'ruled' by the Goddess of love:Venus.

Scorpio Ascendant

Scorpio is another Water sign, intense and deep and usually in a crowd or company will appear quiet and withdrawn. It's another strong Asc for a Pisces to have and can tend to suspicion at the worst and transformation at the best. Pisces with a Scorpio Asc looks at life through glasses that peer deep into people's souls, and will pursue a path that will leave others by the wayside as they focus intently of their goals. Make sure you don't get on the wrong side of this Asc-because the backlash can be severe. On the positive side, they are great achievers.

Sagittarius Ascendant

Sagittarius is another Fire sign and wants to travel, be free, philosophize, learn, teach, be in foreign cultures. As long as there are no ties and plenty of rope, Sag Asc Pisces will generally look at life in a positive, upbeat, happy manner. This is quite a cheerful Asc and as such helps Pisces from slipping too deeply into negative spaces, provided they've 'found their path' and their beliefs are acknowledged.

Capricorn Ascendant

"Living the life of a Pisces is complicated. I am a Pisces with a Capricorn ascendant.

Touched by many, many hard life experiences. I don't do sympathy but am totally empathic probably due to life's lessons."

Capricorn is another Earth sign and ruled by Saturn makes a challenging Asc for a Pisces because it can make the individual negative and always fearing the worst. The plus side is life gets better as they get older, as they learn that age and experience are valuable assets. It does makes a Pisces very sensible having this as an Asc and they may be drawn to have friends that are older than them.

Aquarius Ascendant

Aquarius is an Air sign, ruled by wacky Uranus, the planet of rebellion. Their deep desire is for friendship and they want to be friends with everybody. Not just chummy friends but friends they can play with, do interesting things with and be part of something bigger like 'Save the Earth'. It can make them a little colder than other combinations and more critical but on the plus side, their diaries are full and their Xmas card list, long.

Pisces Ascendant

"I'm a Pisces. I have no siblings, an absent father and an absent mother). I don't feel I fit in the world. I don't feel I belong here. I have never been able to 'fit in'."

Pisces is as we have discussed a Water sign and with a Pisces Ascendant will make a Pisces even more of a Pisces.

If the Ascendant is in the same sign as the Sun-sign, they *are* that sign. This is called a 'Double Pisces' because the outside and the inside are the same. Their view and their self are similar. However, Pisces Ascendant can be drawn into addictions and dependencies and feel empathy to everyone's hard-luck story. If your child or partner has this combination, they need space on their own, gentle handling and lots of time dreaming, and sleeping. This combination can sleep for England!

Chapter Four

The Moon

With our example chart we've discovered that Einstein has a Cancer Ascendant now we're going to learn about the Moon. On the circle of the chart on the right-hand side you'll see the glyph for The Moon, and it's in section (house) number 6. Next to the Moon symbol you will see the number 14. This means Einstein's Moon is 14% in the sign of Sagittarius. Now read on for what the Moon means.

The Moon
The Moon in Astrology represents how we feel about things. If the Sun is who we are, and the Ascendant is how we project ourselves, then the Moon is how we respond emotionally to things.

The difference between a thought and a feeling is: a thought is something that happens swiftly and comes from our minds, a feeling happens just after the thought and comes from our heart. If you hit me, I might think ' blimey, why did she do that?' then the feeling of pain in my jaw would follow, then the emotion of sadness or anger, depending on how my chart is constructed. But in any given situation, there will be a thought, then an emotion, and that emotion is the Moon.

In reality the Moon changes sign every 2 days or so, and if you ever want to do an interesting experiment, read the headlines of the daily papers and pay attention to the Moon signs.

On an Aries-Moon day, more people are fighting, on a Cancer-Moon day, more about the home , on a Pisces-Moon day, maybe weird and wonderful and inexplicable mysteries. Try it, you'll be surprised.

So the Moon 'rules' how we feel and some Moons are easier to handle for Pisces than others. I have included the Dr Edward Bach Flower Essences that match the Moon sign, as most people are fine about 'who' they are but the Moon represents the subconscious and occasionally needs a little bit of support.

You know how it is, you want to leave your job and you hate your boss and your Sun in Sagittarius is happy to leave. But have you run this past your Moon in Taurus, that is worried you'll starve to death and become penniless? So all that happens is, you keep saying you want to do something but it never happens. I recommend if you're stuck somewhere in your life find out the sign of your Moon and have a little chat with it and see if it's happy to do what you want. The subconscious is like a child and believes everything it's told. The Bach Flower Essences help the Moon to feel less scared and worried. I use them a lot in my practice.

The Dr Bach Flower Essences

In 1933 Dr Edward Bach a medical doctor and Homeopath published a little booklet called 'The Twelve Healers and other remedies'. His theory was that if the emotional component a person was suffering from was removed, their 'illness' would also disappear. I tend to agree with this kind of thinking as most illnesses (except being hit by a car) are preceded by an unhappy event or an emotional disruption that then sets into place the body getting out of sync. Removing the emotional issue and bringing a bit of stability into someone's life, when they are 'all over the place' certainly doesn't hurt and in some cases can improve the overall health so much that wellness resumes.

Knowing which Bach Flower Essence can help certain worries and upsets gives your Pisces more control over their lives (and yours if you are in the vicinity) and I've quoted Dr Bach's actual words for each sign.

To use the Essences take 2 drops from the stock bottle and put it into a glass of water and sip. I tend to recommend putting them into a small water bottle, and sipping them through-out the day, at least 4 times. For young children, do the same.

Remember to seek medical attention if symptoms don't get better and/or seek professional counselling.

Aries Moon

"I am one and loving it."

An Aries Moon will want all their needs met, to feel cared for, loved for who they are and for what they do, as Aries is an action sign. They feel better having everything they need, right here, right now. Patience won't wash. Aries Moon processes their emotions by action, lots of it. Running, jumping, physical expression is good but however their Moon operates, it will be swift, fast and immediate. Like a storm, it will all seem very spectacular and invigorating, then in a few moments, the storm will pass, and they'll be back to their friendly selves.Their feelings are expressed powerfully and impetuously, and they may find it hard to distance themselves from them. The most obvious benefit of this is the honesty of their gut reaction to events.

Bach Flower Essence Impatiens:

'Those who are quick in thought and action and who wish all things to be done without hesitation or delay.'

Taurus Moon

"And I must have a fast metabolism. I do eat. I eat with the kids...and I eat after the kids too! People always look amazed when I start wolfing it down." Patsy Kensit (Pisces Moon in Taurus)

Taurus Moon will need their emotional needs to be met by sensuality, fine food, fine wine, luxurious silks and satins. Their Moon is slower, and takes time to respond. They feel through having their bellies filled and their finances stable. A good meal and a cheque from the boss will calm most Taurus Moon fears. Taurean fixity makes them an emotionally consistent person, slow to change their heart but they should beware of hanging onto out-dated feelings. In a crisis some Taurus Moons will not be able to *do* anything. They have to stop and think and 'let it all sink in'. If their steady, slow progress is interrupted by some obstacle, they get down-hearted and discouraged.

Bach Flower Essence Gentian:

'Those who are easily discouraged. They may be progressing well in the affairs of their daily life, but any small delay or hindrance to progress causes doubt and soon disheartens them'

Gemini Moon

"We would get writers and things like that and whatever contribution I could make, in with the writers — if I thought of a good joke or I thought up a good piece of business, I would contribute that" Zeppo Marx (Pisces Moon in Gemini)

Oh Gemini Moon, they're not so easy to placate! As long as they have 15 different people to discuss their issues with, 12 self-help books and a focus for their changeable emotions, they're fine. Gemini is such an airy, abstract energy, they are likely to analyse and rationalise their emotions more than the average. The plus side of this is the clarity of self-knowledge, the minus is that they may end up simply worrying about it all too much. Sometimes the answer to the problem may be to simply turn off the brain for a while. One thing is for sure, during an emotional crisis, the Gemini Moon's phone-bill goes through the roof.

This Essence comes under the heading 'For Those Who Suffer Uncertainty' (which Libra and Gemini both suffer from.)

Bach Flower Essence Cerato:

'Those who have not sufficient confidence in themselves to make their own decisions'

Cancer Moon

"I knew I was different. I thought that I might be gay or something because I couldn't identify with any of the guys at all. None of them liked art or music, they just wanted to fight and get laid." Kurt Cobain (Pisces, Moon in Cancer)

As the sign Cancer is 'ruled' by the Moon, their emotional self is happy in this sign. They might find they are influenced by the sign the Moon is in during the week, so get a good Moon calendar and pay attention to what sign the Moon is in. It does stack-up the water content in their chart, because Cancer is a Water sign and makes them prone to holding onto emotions they should have let go of years ago, but overall it makes them extra sensitive to others emotional needs. Astrology regards this as a highly 'maternal' influence, their emotions will be well tuned to protecting and nurturing others.

Bach Flower Essence Clematis:

'Living in the hopes of happier times, when their ideals may come true.'

Leo Moon

"I find other signs are drawn by our deepness - even if we frustrate them to death afterwards!!! We do it all in such a cute way though that we get away with it!"

Leo Moon is a contradiction for a Pisces. A Moon that wants recognition, when the Moon really wants to be in the background. Their emotional needs are best met when someone can recognise their need to feel thanked and respected and sometimes even praised. They have the ability to react swiftly to emotional situations and as a Fixed Fire sign feel best having special moments and 'me time'. Red carpets wouldn't be amiss either.....Leo's traditional love of being in the limelight means that Moon-in-Leo people are likely to have an instinct for being the centre of attention.

Bach Flower Essence Vervain:

'Those with fixed principles and ideas, which they are confident are right'.

Virgo Moon

"The PMDD, Pre-menstrual Dysphoric Disorder turns my already chaotic life upside down. It's like PMS x 1000. I turn into a different person. My perception changes, I fly off in rages, I can't do my normal tasks, I feel like a burden to everyone around me. I am on Prozac and trying to follow a healthy diet and plenty of exercise to combat the moods, but the winter is hard and I'm not coping very well at the moment, even with the Prozac. Some days I really do wonder why I am here."

Now a Pisces with Moon in Virgo has their emotional self a long distance from their ego self. Virgo is the opposite sign to Pisces and their challenge is to *not* fret about things, *not* worry themselves to a frenzy and learnt to trust that everything will work out OK. Virgo Moons are good at absorbing feelings, rationalising them, then turning them out like a lovely birthday cake. Their only problem is when there is too much to deal with, then they become the rabbit frozen in the headlights. Virgo Moons are often seen as somewhat challenging because Virgo wants order and harmony and that proves difficult when emotions take over. Consequently they might try and keep their emotions tightly organised...which only results in them popping-up without warning.

My most often prescribed remedy, as Virgo Moon, Sun and Asc are my best customers. It comes under the heading 'Over-Sensitive to Influences and Ideas'.

Bach Flower Essence Centaury:

'Their good nature leads them to do more than their own share of work and they may neglect their own mission in life.'

Libra Moon

"I've lived alone for most of the past 6 years, climbing the walls every

evening with frustration and loneliness."

Pisces with a Libra Moon does need people. Friendly, loving people that don't argue or swear. They love beauty and shades of pastel and as long as they can connect with others who can appreciate their gentle genteelness they're fine. How everyone gets on with everyone else is a major concern, and their partner will, if they're not careful, become a major focus in life. On a down day they have problems making up their mind and can sway from one idea to another. Libran energy puts a strong emphasis on harmony and balance. The fear of expressing emotions which may cause difficult scenes means that Moon-Librans may say one thing while secretly feeling and doing something else. As a Pisces they also long for a partner and would rather be in a bad relationship, than not in one at all.

Bach Flower Essence Scleranthus:

'Those who suffer from being unable to decide between two things, first one seeming right then the other.'

Scorpio Moon

"There'll come a time when most of us return here, Brought back by our desire to be, A perfect entity, Living through a million years of crying ,Until you've realized the Art of Dying, Do you believe me?" The Art of Dying, George Harrison(Pisces Moon in Scorpio)

Scorpio is a strong Moon for Pisces to have and one that can absorb a large amount of negative energy without falling apart. Their feelings are intense, fixed and deep. Their emotional needs are not light and fluffy like Gemini, or practical like Taurus, they reside somewhere deep like a cavern or underground volcano. They can be tense and if they want something, by hook or by crook, they'll get it. The word 'deep' recurs in astrological descriptions of this combination: deep longings, deep passions. Consequently, when things don't go to plan a Pisces with Moon in Scorpio will project all their disappointments onto the outside world. I don't often see this combination as most of the time they can manage in life and are quite self-sufficient. Trust is extremely important to them. It you want someone to help the under-dog this is the sign combination that is wonderful for that.

This Essence comes under the heading: ' Over-Care for Welfare Of Others'

Bach Flower Essence Chicory:

'They are continually correcting what they consider wrong and enjoy doing so.'

Sagittarius Moon

"Before God we are all equally wise - and equally foolish." Albert Einstein(Pisces Moon in Sagittarius)

Pisces with a Sagittarius moon makes for quite an unusual combination. Sagittarius is so famed for putting their foot in their mouth and saying what others only think, while Pisces is the sign of watching and waiting and observing. So there their Moon is, wanting answers, reasons, and a nice long trip to Outer Mongolia, friendly, sociable and philosophical. Their emotions are ruled by upbeat, benevolent Jupiter and this gives them a trusting and positive outlook on life and people. Moon-in-Sagittarians always bounce back and never lose their funda-mental faith in humanity. As a Fire sign it also gives this Pisces the chance of action, something most Pisces find hard to do.

This Essence comes under the heading 'Over-Sensitive to Influences and Ideas'. Reading something upsetting will influence them a great deal.

Bach Flower Essence Agrimony:

'They hide their cares behind their humor and jesting and try to bear their trials with cheerfulness.'

Capricorn Moon

"The three most celebrated doctors on the island have seen me. One sniffed as what I spat, the second tapped where I spat, the third listened as I spat. The first said I was dead, the second said I'm dying, the third

said I'm going to die." Frederic Chopin (Pisces Moon in Capricorn)

Of the Moon signs Capricorn is probably the most challenging. It is ruled by scary Saturn, the grim reaper and planet of hard knocks, so their emotional make-up is severe and self-flagellating. Like Scorpio Moon they can absorb more negativity than other signs but it makes them fearful of more pain. "Stop beating yourself up" would be a good motto. Capricorn is above all signs concerned with the tough material reality of the world, while the Moon is the 'inner child' and can make the individual seem emotionally harsh. This however, is only a compensation for wanting to be realistic about life. Capricorn Moons also have *so* many fears which can make them afraid to do anything.

Bach Flower Essence Mimulus:

'Fear of worldly things, illness, pain, accident, poverty, of dark, of being alone, of misfortune. They secretly bear their dread and do not speak freely of it to others'

Aquarius Moon

"People have these perceptions of you until you somehow are lucky enough to break them." Glenn Close, Actress (Pisces Moon in Aquarius)

Now I have come across a number of Pisces with Aquarius Moons, and you'd never know they were Pisces. That Aquarius flavour makes them *so* detached from their emotions that they almost become a 'normal' person. Air signs don't do emotions very well, they prefer to think rather than feel and can become overwhelmed if too much water rains on them!The squidgy Pisces Sun sits next to the rational, free-thinking Aquarius Moon and depending on what year they were born, either increases or decreases their ability to keep their life on track. They may find their emotions hard to get to grips with as Aquarian energy is airy and gives them a natural tendency to consider them in an abstract way. Equally, it is a fixed energy, and emotions are famously fluid and hard to pin down. The result is they are very unlikely to wear their heart on their sleeve and may seem cool and unpredictable.

Bach Flower Essence Water Violet:

'For those who like to be alone, very independent, capable and self-reliant. They are aloof and go their own way.'

Pisces Moon

"Often things only become clear to me after the fact, so I just "go with the flow" of my intuition.

I once read 'the Pisces female will buy a biscuit tin to put candles in'. This made me laugh, because I had done exactly that."

Now if you've read this far well done and if you've skipped to just read this section I need to add a disclaimer here and now.

If you're involved with a Pisces with a Pisces Moon, take a deep breath and exaggerate and magnify everything I've said about Pisces so far. This makes for an especially sensitive soul and if your Pisces is a boy *please* treat him gently. He's not going to be a politician or a pop-star (if he does he might get into drugs, Kurt Cobain is a good example) he'll certainly be creative, musical, inspired, talented *but* he might not know what day of the week it is, where he put his watch, wallet, money or bus-fare unless he is cared for in a Steiner-type environment that takes his gentleness into account. Pisces is the most intrinsically emotional of the signs and can have access to acute emotional sensitivity, which makes life complicated, and action difficult so they can end up being the famous Piscean fish out of water. There is certainly an astrological consensus that this is the sign of the martyr, and awareness of suffering, but as the 12th sign, they should also be uniquely placed to resolve all emotions, hence Moon-in-Pisces is often seen as a combination giving mystical insight.

This Essence comes under the heading 'For Those Who Have Fear' and will help this fragile, gentle soul take courage to face any emergency be it death of a beloved pet to starting school.

Bach Flower Essence Rock Rose:

'For cases where there even appears no hope or when the person is very frightened or terrified.'

Chapter Five

The Houses

In our example, Einstein has his Pisces Sun in the 9th house. Top right in the wheel in section number 9.

Here we have what each house means. The houses represent an area of life. Each house is different and over the years the meaning of the houses has stayed pretty constant, as Astrologers today, still make correlations between the 'movement' of the planets and what is happening with their clients in their practices. There is also plenty of disagreement amongst Astrologers to what is the best method to employ to categorise someone. There are different house systems, Placidus being the one most Astrologers use today, because that's the one that Astrology computer programmes use.

I use a programme designed for the general public (rather than Astrologers) because it's then easier for my clients to understand what is happening, and I can avoid jargon, and losing them.

The system I use is called 'Equal House' because all the houses are of equal size, and is incidentally, the first house system ever used....and I like the idea if it ain't broke don't fix it, and equal house is easy and I'm all for easy, aren't you?

For the purposes of this book, all we need is the most important parts of the chart, the building block if you will, of Asc, Sun, Moon and house the Sun is in.

So here we have a brief introduction to the houses and their meanings. Please remember, I didn't decide what each house means (!) it was developed over years of observation and experimentation by Astrologers. If you want to learn about the history of Astrology I recommend relevant books in the appendix.

So, the houses.

These are the present day accepted meanings of each house written as if your Pisces has their Sun in one of those various houses. The Sun is *how* we shine, the house is *where* we prefer to shine.

This is one part of Astrology that most people get the most confused about. What is a 'house'? It's a mathematical division of the circle. The Asc, as we have learned, is deduced by the time of birth, the houses are the circle divided into 12.

Astrologers haven't always made charts in a circle, they've also been made into squares, divided into 12 segments but if you ask me, a circle seems to make more sense and with making a chart into a square, you then miss the lovely shapes that the planets can make around the circle.

One thing is for sure, a birth chart does represent the position of the planets, on the day of birth, in the different constellations in the sky. But I know a lot of people who look at a chart and wonder that the hell it all *means*.

So, a house is the circle divided anti-clockwise into 12 segments. Each segment represents a different 'area' of life from how others see you, to how you see yourself and everything in between.

Over the years the 'houses' haven't really changed much in what they represent. What luckily has got lost over the centuries is the horrible scary terminology used to describe parts of a chart. Words like 'Lord of' ....and the 'Benefic' and 'Malefic' planets implying if you had a Malefic planet in your chart, death and destruction would be the result. If you read old chart interpretations, you could quite easily feel scared about your health and wellbeing with some of the things that got written.

Now, just to make things complicated there are about 5 or more house 'systems' that are used. The most popular one in all the computer programmes is called 'Placidus' but that is only because all the old books were written using it and it wasn't used in the UK until the 18th century. The 'system' used before this is the Equal House System, the one that I prefer and in fact enjoy using.

The Equal House System uses the Ascendant as cusp 1 and then divides the whole zodiac into 12 equal parts for the 12 'houses'. I have put in brackets what Ascendant Sun in each house should have because in the Equal House System there is a choice of two.

The Placidus system takes into account far more complicated data such as how long it takes for the Earth to move so that we 'see' different sections of the Zodiac from earth, which in a nutshell, means each 'house' of the chart is a different size.

Why make things complicated is my question? Life is complicated enough already, so if you're using a computer programme or an Internet site, please check which system is being used and change it to Equal House.

Easy!

The First House, House of Personality

Female Pisces, Aquarius Asc, Sun in the first, Moon in Aries

"I am one and loving it. I love my fantasy life and am creative, acting, writing (poetry mostly but am attempting a novel based on a time in my life), love the water, astrology, nature...especially rocks (gemology and Earth Science major). And am a very intuitive and spiritual being. I am told I have an unstoppable positive attitude and am always happy but if I am accused confrontationally about something I didn't do, look out! There is a quick flash temper in defending myself...but as quickly over with."

The first house comes straight after the Ascendant and is almost *the* most important house and is of equal significance to the Sun or Moon signs. Temperament, personality, health are all expressed here, it is the 'character' of the person..A Pisces with a Pisces first house and their Sun in that first house will normally be born around 6am-8am in the morning. Their boundaries will be weak and they will pick-up other people's moods like a radar. They know who they are most of the time, as long as the people who they are with are weaker but if the other character is stronger, Pisces becomes a mirror for them or even can 'become' them. Having a first house Sun makes the native quite self-assured, the Pisces Sun in the first will illuminate the 'self'. It makes this type of Pisces easy to understand, what you see is what you get. Depending on their Moon sign, they should be quite confident, as is the lady above. Her Moon is in Aries so it also makes her fearless. One thing I have noticed with people who have Sun in the first is, they are the most important person in their world. In an Aries way, their focus will always be on 'me'.

(Asc Pisces or Aries)

The Second House, House of Money, Material Possessions and Self-Worth

"My core principles are steadfast and trying to change them can take a lot of convincing, but I keep trying and it will usually work."

The second house rules our first relations with the outer world. It covers material things, money and possessions, security and stability. If these sound like Taurus keywords, that's because each house from 1-12 is like each sign of the Zodiac, and the 2nd house is like Taurus. It's the balance between the attitude to material goods (e.g. hard cash) and spiritual goods such as love and friends and also the sense of self-worth. Piscean energy is not immediately tuned in to the 2nd house which concerns money and material things. This can mean that they seek deeper meanings behind money etc. The clients I have met with Sun in the 2nd, are concerned with the practical side of life. Money, their house, their job, how much they are 'worth'. Pisces with Sun in the 2nd will need to sort out pretty early in life, their financial situation, otherwise with this placement will forever be working against themselves. They need the building blocks of life firmly in place. An income, a job, a house, money in the bank. I'm sure you get the picture!

(Asc Aquarius or Capricorn).

The Third House, House of Communication & Short Journeys

The third house rules learning to speak and think, relations with close relatives, especially brothers or sisters, and short journeys. Gemini's connection with the mind also means that planetary influences here in the third house may well make the individual liable to change their mind a lot. Pisces is very concerned with oneness and wholeness, whilst the 3rd house is about dividing, organizing and comparing separate things. The Pisces Sun here gives intuitive insights into rational processes and helps a Pisces be more rational and communicative. I have found that clients with Sun in the 3rd have enormous phone-bills and just love to chat for the sake of it, so if you have a little Pisces, don't get them a mobile phone too early unless you can negotiate a cheap or free amount of air time. 3rd house natives also need to feel 'heard' so listen to their views and opinions, you don't have to agree but you do have to listen.

(Asc Capricorn or Sagittarius).

The Fourth House, House of Home, Family & Roots

The fourth house covers the home and domestic life in general and is influenced by Cancer home-loving qualities. As Cancer is ruled by the Moon, this house also describes relations with the mother or maternal figure, but it is also seen as covering attitudes to both parents, and to 'roots' in general . Pisces Sun in the 4th house indicates that inner peace and stability will be family-oriented in some way and may find expression in less obvious ways - like treating friends or work colleagues as though they are part of a big family. Coming to terms with up-bringing and roots certainly helps Pisces Sun in the 4th have a more happy life. I always recommend 4th house Sun clients to do their family tree and make peace with their past. Healing Your Family Patterns by David Furlong[6] certainly helps here. Another interesting thing I've noticed with Indigo Children with Sun in the 4th is they really respond well to home schooling, so if your little Pisces is Sun in the 4th consider this as an option.

(Asc Sagittarius or Scorpio).

The Fifth House, House of Creativity & Romance

Female Pisces, Libra Asc, Sun in the 5th, Moon in Pisces in the 5th

"I am a Pisces Sun and Moon, with government documented psychic abilities since I was a child. I believe I tend to receive, as opposed to send, impressions-although if I make a conscious effort (which I usually don't) I can also send a message for someone to call me that I'm having difficulty reaching."

The fifth house covers the desire to make a mark in the wider world. and could be anything creative or active 'out there' - cooking, playing, love affairs, gambling or partying. Like Leo who loves to be the center of attention, Pisces Sun in the 5th loves Creativity with a capital 'C'. I've met so many people with Sun in the 5th who really should promote themselves more. Pisces Sun here demands respect for the products of their creation, be they children, Art (with a capital 'A') poetry, performing skills, film, TV, or the more toned-down 'things-I-have-made-myself'. If your little one has this, make sure you put their creations on display somewhere in the house. Maybe a notice-board in the kitchen? Older Pisces will love to be 'included' in whatever is 'in fashion' at the moment. They will also enjoy the thrill of the chase more than what has been caught, so don't automatically expect them to want to settle down too early.

(Asc Scorpio or Libra)

The Sixth House, House of Work & Health

Female Virgo Asc, Sun in the 6th, Moon in Libra in the 1st.

"I find it hard to be organized and structured, to make decisions and create goals in my life. I tend to be erratic and to withdraw from the limelight. I make myself small. Apparently I am hard to hold and to meet (according to my tutor, diploma in counseling still at it -what a mug!)... However, people see me has calm, patient and caring... and find me a good listener/healing...they just don't seem to expect that I may want to be heard, supported or listened to as well."

The sixth house governs health and what work we do and I've found clients with this placement who are happiest when they have a caring job or doing volunteer work. They must also master the art of tidiness, something a lot of Pisces struggle with. Once they've got that under their belt things improve. So boxing things up, putting things away, and finding places for everything is beneficial. Mind you, I know plenty of Virgos who are the messiest people alive, so the Virgo influence isn't about tidiness per se, but about putting things in their place. Being able to categorize things. Feeling ordered. Virgo influence also carries constant worries, so they can easily be reduced by making concrete plans, by making lists, by writing things down and keeping accurate records. The lady above is a therapist and when she learned how to relax (through hypnotherapy) she then was able to expand her massage practice and organize teaching workshops.

(Asc Libra or Virgo).

The Seventh House, House of Relationships & Marriage

The seventh house now turns from the 'inner' concerns of the individual, psychological needs and attitudes, to the important

'outer' concerns of society and relationships. It focuses on the desire for partnership, and, ruled by Venus, on important loves. This is traditionally the marriage house, so the subject of marriage will be important to 7th house Pisces and gives a deep sense of union and connection with a partner/lover and for profound closeness. I can agree with these statements as I have Sun in the 7th and my close personal relationships have influenced my development as a person. Finding my soul-love was the most uplifting experience for me and one that made everything else 'fall into place'. Clients I see with this placement or with planets in Libra are generally given the prescription of 'find a loving partner', and their lives improve. That's not to say they can't function without one, they just feel more 'at home'.
(Asc Virgo or Leo).

The Eighth House, House of Life Force in Birth, Sex, Death & the After-Life

The eighth house can be described as the home of the 'life force' covering intense experiences such as sex, death, transformation, reincarnation, and 'born again' religious experiences. What happens in the eighth house is deep and important. Scorpio is the sign of intensity so Pisces with an 8th house Sun is more likely to be secretive, more likely to want to control their internal environment (and maybe their partners too). They want to delve deeply into life's experiences. They will stop at nothing once their mind is focused on 'the way ahead' and they can spend all their energies on things we might not even understand, or want to know about. Imagine a secret society, this is the sort of thing an 8th house Sun will want to involve themselves in.

This house also rules financial investments, insurance policies etc. 'other people's money'. Sex is extremely important to this combination as is Pisces desire to lose themselves in others. I don't see too many Pisces clients in practice with this combination as it makes them very strong emotionally and less likely to seek help....I tend to see their partners.

(Asc Leo or Cancer).

The Ninth House, House of Philosophy & Long Distance Travel

This house rules travel and foreign languages, and also over the various 'inner' journeys, spiritual or philosophical, that may be engaged in. It also covers higher education, dreams and ideals. Pisces has an irresistible association with grand mystical projects to understand the meaning of life and everything, and that is very much the territory covered by the 9th house, so crazy (to others) theories come easily. All Pisces with this combination will want to travel the world, meet other cultures, explore distant lands literally by getting on a plane or by reading about them or surfing the Internet. The 9th house Pisces clients I see are always 'on a mission' to find their spiritual self- so they can amass large quantities of spiritual reading material.

They can also be blunt sometimes to the point of rudeness, but their insights are true and shouldn't be ignored. OK if you're a Leo you'll struggle with their honesty but what's the good in hiding behind politeness would be this person's mantra? Younger Pisces will want to ride as the 9th house is ruled by Sagittarius and Jupiter and as we know Sagi was the half-man half-horse Centaur. I know little Pisces kiddies who can't manage a week without riding or being in contact with horses. In fact I read for a lady once who was a healer who used horses for this then progressed to wild animals, but her first work was with horses. The pull is very strong.

(Asc Cancer or Gemini).

The Tenth House, House of Social Identity & Career

The tenth house is ruled by steady and practical Capricorn and is most easily and commonly abbreviated to being the 'career house'. Ambitions and worldly progress are expressed here as well as financial value. This house also covers Authority in all its forms, how people react to it, how they deal with having authority over others. The tenth is generally seen as a pretty hard headed and practical part of our chart - our careers, whilst Pisces tends to inject the mystical and dreamy into things. This combination is a little difficult consequently 10th house Pisces will want a 'career' but might take all their life to find the one that fits the bill. 10th house Pisces Sun's are concerned with 2 things: what others think or say about them and 'where am I going?' in their careers. The plus side is as life goes on, they become more focused on their goals and more able to achieve them.If they were only to work with their heart energy, not their head, they'd find their lives a little easier.

(Asc Gemini or Taurus).

The Eleventh House, House of Social Life & Friendships

The eleventh house covers aspirations , social conscience, social life and a wide circle of friends in true Aquarian style. Altruism, Ecology, Friendship and 'Save The Planet' is written high in the sky for this house for Pisces. They enjoy being part of a group, building ideas, working in a team and sharing resources. They will worry about the planet, their friends, their friends-of-friends and will want everyone to join hands and work for a common purpose. If you want someone to support your cause, this is the ideal combination to ask. If you want them to work on their own for any length of time, they will soon get upset. They love societies, clubs, charities, groups and anything that connects them with others for an altruistic purpose.

(Asc Taurus or Aries).

The Twelfth House, House of Spirituality

The twelfth is all about mystical stuff we can't really understand. It makes the native shy and less likely to want to be in the limelight and as they can have an Aries Asc, there is the terrible dilemma of wanting to be seen.....and then wanting to hide away. If they have a Pisces Asc, then they will be very happy just being in the background, playing with the fairies, dreaming the night away and not really being in the planet. The positive note is these are souls with many past lives, so if you want someone to give you mystical insights, look them up. On the negative side they can just as easily slip into drugs and drink so if this is your child, please teach them practical skills to help them cope with life on the planet.

(Asc Aries or Pisces).

So, in our example we're just dealing with Einstein's personality, not how his life turned out. We have someone who is basically rather shy. A Cancer Ascendant is not famed for rushing into things and will want money and finances to be stable. When Einstein married his first wife Mileva he chose well as she was a Sagittarius with her Moon in Virgo, so they had a Moon/Sun connection. If you remember Einstein had his Moon in Sag.............anyway, Sagi Moon is good for being involved in philosophy and he had his Sun in the 9th, so that doubles the Sag influence because the 9th house is the same as the 9th sign........but this is a book about Pisces not about Einstein. Suffice to say, I expect he died quite a happy man because he managed to achieve what he set out to do against quite a lot of opposition and he just trundled along doing what he loved. And there's the rub, if you do what you love, everything else falls into place.

As this book is called how to survive a Pisces, I'm now going to give you instruction in how to do just that.

Chapter Six

The Problems

Be firm

Be gentle

Be compassionate

That's it! What more do I need to say?.........but, I can hear you wail. My Pisces says he loves me but he can't forget his last girlfriend and he's still grieving for his mother and he can't get the job he wants because he needs 10 more years training and he hasn't got enough money for that and his drink problem is getting worse because I'm not earning enough........and ....STOP!!

Already you are living the Pisces' life. They're quite capable of living their own lives. They don't need advice. They need guidance and they need it delivered in a way they can understand.

Let me give you some examples:

Your Pisces won't commit

Simple. Your Pisces doesn't love you. If he did, he'd be using his last penny to buy you a ring and take you on a walk through glistening streets with the Moon shining on you and pointing out stars and sounds you never thought were there.

He likes you. He loves your teeth, your hair, some of your clothes, your Mother's home-made pies, your paintings, your singing voice, but he doesn't love you. A Pisces in love will stop at nothing to make that love as romantic and enjoyable as possible.

The truth is, he doesn't know how to tell you. He can't find the words to say it. He looks at the situation, that's if he ever looks at it at all, with such rose-tinted spectacles,worrying that if he told you he didn't love you, you'd throw out his cat and burn his photos and be depressed and unhappy for years and years and years...........but he isn't happy, because when Pisces ARE happy, they just melt into the background and observe and linger. When they're unhappy, everyone else suffers, and the world becomes a bitter place.

Don't try and make a Pisces *do* anything. You're wasting your time. Don't tell them stuff. Their poor minds are already filled with so many people's anguish.

That woman you poured your heart out to at the bus-stop or in the pub or in the supermarket, was probably a Pisces. They're always on duty. Soaking up the sorrows of life and trying to prevent more suffering. They don't like pain. Even the ones with Aries Moons, or Capricorn Ascendants.

The quickest way to make a Pisces switch off, is to make them watch suffering on the telly. They can feel more than you've ever felt, sense more than a bloodhound, but ask them to calculate logarithms and you're in for a hard time.

We need Pisces. We need all the signs of the Zodiac and Pisces is the last sign. The one that has been through all the incarnations before. It doesn't make them more knowledgeable or more worthy, it just makes them, sometimes, more tired. More exhausted. "Do I HAVE to do this life time again?",a lot of Pisces ask? 'Do I HAVE to marry and have children and get a job and drive a car and smile.......when all I want to do is sleep and dream and settle and fill in the gaps?'

If your Pisces won't commit, then finish the relationship ASAP.

Your Pisces doesn't know if she loves you
Tricky one this. Sometimes direct questioning isn't the best idea.If she tells you that she dreams about you, thinks about you, likes your jokes (even laughs at them!) doodles your name by the

phone, paints you a picture, makes you a cake, wants you to go to a psychic event with her, she probably loves you. If she writes you a song or a poem even better. You get my drift. The love will be subtle, non-direct and mostly gentle.

Sometimes Pisces have a difficulty expressing exactly how they *do* feel. After all, if your ruling planet was Neptune, you'd understand. He's such a slippery fish and so difficult to describe or pin-down. Liz Greene[13] has done a fabulous job describing in true Virgo-detailed style the ins and out of Neptune ....but I feel Neptune is more about those moments when you just 'are' and unless you've taken loads of drugs or been away with the fairies, then that's a hard place to describe.

The 'are' is same as 'is'. You're existing. There is no pain. Nothing feels good...............or bad but there is a connection and it's the connection that Pisces longs for. Sometimes they find it by being creative. Sometimes it comes in moments they're not expecting. Like on a bus or when washing-up. A connection to everything they need to have. That everything they want is provided for, there are no worries, nothing hurts.

Like when you watch a bird in the wild and you can feel the wind slowly blowing you the same way the bird is flying and you know that same wind is with the bird..............and you. Most Pisces like sleep because sleep brings re-connection to the dream-world, and the dream-world doesn't judge or say 'No' too much.

I can close my eyes and slowly drift into sleep, anywhere, anytime. It takes me about 5 minutes normally to go to sleep. I close my eyes and focus 'in the distance' and I can see a path through a wood or a building (most of my dreams are about buildings at the moment). They're not vivid images. They're the same colour as the back of my eyes......but as I relax and get interested in what might lie there, I move into the image and start taking part in what's going on. All this is far more interesting than the clock ticking, or noises outside, the lure of what's in these images is stronger than where I'm lying. The pull to be in a dream world is far stronger than the one to be outside in the 'real' world. All Pisces can do this and some can describe it better than others.

So if your Pisces doesn't know if she loves you, read between the lines. Look for the evidence. The little subtle pointers that show she does.

My Pisces is hopeless with money

Now this seems to affect all Pisces of both genders. Money will be classified by them as the route of all evil, so it's best if you re-educate them on this subject, but add a spiritual spin. If a Pisces thinks that extra cash can be spent on doing good, or benefiting others (other than themselves) they are quite capable of accruing vast amounts. Even better if they read something by Stuart Wilde as he covers the spiritual aspects of money, which our fishy friends need to know. It's also best to have a separate bank account from them, as your joint money might easily be 'squandered' on some charitable outlet or used to help someone *much* worse off than you..........Credit cards and loans unless short-term and affordable aren't the best ways to tackle Pisces money difficulties, but practical, sorted, down-to-earth advice, from a nice Earth sign bank manager always does well.

My Pisces says he loves me *and* someone else and can't choose between us

This is more Gemini territory, but Pisces will invariably, at sometime in their life, experience this problem.

The best way to deal with it, is to be realistic about what love is. You can't love two people at once, in a romantic way, because love is all about being exclusive. Maybe if your Pisces has Uranus near their sun (which last happened in 1921) or in their 7th house, maybe, but I don't rate two-timing as a good thing. Be firm. Tell your Pisces that you will walk away from this relationship and only return when they decide to practice monogamy. What might be causing your Pisces the difficulty, is you making things too easy for them. So make it harder all round, then pat yourself on the back when your Pisces suddenly realizes they can't live without you.

My Pisces doesn't know what to do with their life

This is a question I am asked regularly. 'What should I be doing with my life'? It might be best to start with what you shouldn't be doing with a life. Worrying about it, for one, is a waste of precious energy. Get a good Astrologer to interpret your chart and see what signs and planets you have in the 6th house of work and the 10th house of career and look even deeper at where the North node is in your chart because this represents where we should be 'going' in this life. Don't expect to get intimate details such as 'working on the food counter in Harrods' or 'buying and selling property in Provence.'

Aim more for working in an environment that allows space and intuition.

And in Astrology, there is a difference between work and career. One is what you do every day, the other is what you work towards. One is the physical process like answering the phone the other is where it is heading and how you 'frame' it. Most Pisces, but not all, feel better having a career and a hobby. In fact the hobby might be more interesting than the career. What is certain is they need time to themselves without someone breathing down their neck to work out what they truly want to do. And it will usually have a creative spin.

My Pisces is all over the place

This one is something that nearly all Pisces will come across at sometime in their life. They wake up one day and their whole world has fallen apart. If they are a bit of a sleepy Pisces, they might not have seen what was coming, which will result in even more grief and anxiety. First things first. Get out the trusty bottle of Ignatia 30c that every Pisces-lover should have handy. Administer one dose to the falling-about Pisces, and provided they're not actually in the middle of an alcoholic stupor, get them sat down in front of a cup of tea to explain the reason for the life crisis. I can (nearly) guarantee you it will be because of a relationship.

Now I don't know if you've heard of these 2 books?

1) The Rules[15]

2) Mars and Venus on a Date[16]

Both of these books should be treated like a Bible in the houses containing Pisces. Here we have simple, easy to understand common sense advice, from Men and Woman who have been there. They're not experts. (Pisces don't have time for experts)but they will guide the Pisces down the 'what to do next road'.

You see, Pisces give of themselves. They are the ultimate martyr, especially if they've got a Virgo Ascendant .

So what sort of things do people complain about, about the Pisces they know? Different things will affect different people in different ways. An Aires might find a Pisces too slow, too indecisive, too hesitant. Gemini's might find Pisces too soppy and sensitive. I once had a disagreement with my ex-husband. My goldfish had died. It had taken quite a few days to expire and I watched it every day, getting less and less able to eat or float until eventually it got stuck behind a rock in its tank and didn't have the energy to escape. It died.

I was pregnant at the time with our son and was (obviously) emotional about just about everything. After the goldfish had died and been disposed of, I decided that I wanted another fish. My ex (a Gemini) and I went to the Aquarium to buy a new fish. A small goldfish. A little life. We ran out of time and my ex got cross when I started to cry because a) my first fish had died and b) we didn't have time to get another one.He just couldn't understand how I could be so upset and tearful over something less than 3 inches long, that doesn't talk, or bark or meow, in fact doesn't 'do' anything.

At that moment in time I felt completely misunderstood but I tell the story to illustrate the differences between the signs.

Gemini wants to breeze around doing interesting things and being 'cerebral'. The Air signs want to connect and contemplate the bigger, maybe meaningful things in life while Pisces sort of chugs along, admiring the view, doing a bit of this and that.....being 'dreamy', being sensitive, seeing the things that others can't see.

So, when we think about the 'problems' the Pisces might cause in your life, also have a think about can you really expect them to 'be' like you if they're so different anyway?

A Taurus might find a Pisces too impractical, too floppy, not able to grasp basic things like food and money. A Cancer might find them not sensitive enough.

"I am just coming to terms with a major break-up from a Pisces, having also fallen out with a best friend of 20 years, also a Pisces. I think Pisces people tend to be highly emotional and certainly indecisive."

Here we have a Cancerian, the most sensitive star sign saying that Pisces are 'highly emotional'. I sometimes think that you notice in others things that are in your 'self'. Maybe this lady is emotional herself and having two sets of emotional people together caused some discontentment. Maybe now, with this book in her hand, she can get the best from the Pisces she might meet in the future.

So, if your Pisces is in a wobbly, emotional, financial and practical mess, start by gently unraveling 'where it all went wrong' and work forwards from that point.

So here is the following advice based on the Pisces you're with.

Chapter Seven

The Solutions

To get the best from your Pisces, you will need to know how to cope with them, and help them sort things out when it all goes 'horribly wrong'.

Each combination will need a different type of help but one thing is for sure all Pisces need time and space before they can feel better about something that has gone wrong. In fact most of them will want to escape in some way, and this is where we get the Pisces that turns to drink or drugs because this seems to help them reduce the feelings they now have to cope with. And the quickest way to drain any Pisces' energies is for some crisis to happen that they can't cope with. They will start to feel bad. Everyday they wake-up the 'situation' will probably have got worse because they are now floundering in some Pisces wobbly mess, sploshing around, wanting to escape everyone and everything.

They won't be able to *decide* what's best ,which will drive the Air signs Libra, Gemini and Aquarius mad:

"They never seem to give a straight answer, and are hard to pin down to making any sort of commitment, responsibility or plan."

They won't want to *do* anything (for fear of making things worse) which will drive the Fire signs Aries, Leo and Sag mad:

"In the following months we developed a leak under the sink, a leaking shower (which was replaced), leak from a central heating drain off pipe, leaking gutter x 2, then last week our new shower started to leak (it had only been in 6 months) and within days our central heating boiler was leaking."

They might also forget to eat/shop/wash-up and at worst look after themselves which will drive the Earth signs Taurus, Virgo and Capricorn equally as mad:

"Please remember to feed the dog and turn-on the cooker."

And if there are any Water signs Cancer, Scorpio or other Pisces around, they will just all lie around weeping and moaning... or crying because the feelings associated with the 'situation' will be the hardest to bear:

"I went through years of being totally numb... not allowing any feelings."

Please keep in mind the above statement, made by a Pisces. It sums-up their biggest problem: their feelings. Unless they feel OK, nothing much else will happen.

So how do you understand a Pisces' feelings?

Well, there are different degrees of feelings and they're not physical. They're emotional. If you take them into account when dealing with your Pisces, life will be a happier place.

Female, Pisces Asc, Sun in the 1st, Moon in Virgo in the 7th

I've always hated being Pisces, yet loved it at the same time!! (Pisces all over eh?) I try to never stand in judgment of people. I HATE lies and secrets, and can sniff a lie a mile off. I give people chances, probably far too many, but I am always wishing I will see the best in people. I do enjoy cultivating the intuition part, the psychic part, the mystical... and love to learn about all religions and faiths.

I find being in a relationship very difficult. I feel as though they need me far more than I need them. I am a bit of a control freak, again, that might be more to do with my upbringing. I am currently in a relationship.He's a Libra. My mother's a Libra. I've always wondered if by getting with him I've unconsciously asked to learn about his and my mother's traits...

My first pregnancy sent me into hell. Panic attacks, anxiety, insomnia, sickness, depression. Postnatal depression obviously followed. My second pregnancy was better, and my second daughter has opened my eyes up to motherhood. I am now a better mother to both my daughters.

I am an artist and very spiritual.I learnt Tarot, Crystals, Runes, trained to Reiki 2, qualified as an aromatherapist after my first child I call myself Pagan, as I celebrate the festivals every year and teach my children about it.

I love learning, I would like to study astrology myself next. I feel it will add another element to my artwork. My favorite thing to draw is mandalas. Although I would call myself a psychedelic artist. I am also an avid photographer. If I could train to do anything, it would be as an Art Therapist, using the Steiner method, rather than the trad art school/hospital route

In this example we have a few things that need to be taken into consideration.

1)This Pisces has a Pisces Asc, so she is *very* sensitive. The smallest thing will upset her, so she would benefit from learning how to protect herself from the harshness in the world. Just because there is pain and suffering in the world doesn't mean you have to actually indulge in it. People with Pisces Asc cope with the world better if they find ways to **protect themselves from other people's feelings.** Judy Hall covers this beautifully in her wonderful book 'The Art of Psychic Protection'.[14] This Pisces will be in a room with unhappy people, then go home and wonder why they are feeling unhappy themselves. They've just absorbed the feelings in the room and without learning strategies to process them, will keep them inside and cause all sorts of horrible illnesses.

2)This Pisces has Moon in Virgo, so she needs to 'serve'. So she's done the right thing in learning how to be a healer, except she's not doing the sort of healing she knows deep inside will benefit her the most: Art Therapy.

3)This Pisces has already had a number of unsuccessful relationships with partners of completely incompatible signs. Pisces and Libra won't gel well in a close personal relationship.

One will want to merge with the unconscious, the other will want to know all the why's and wherefores and reasons and ideas and Pisces can't provide those things. She's also touched on something that I've found repeatedly in practice, the people will marry/date/live-with a person who is the same sign as the parent they have the most issues with, so they can 'work through' those issues in a more detached way. If you ask me, its much easier to avoid the trauma and see a counsellor about your parental issues than try and make a relationship work because of them.

Here are a few suggestions for the Pisces in your life, if they have an Asc or Moon in these signs

So when they hit that spot of conflict or you find they are not able to cope you will be there to help them through.

Aries Asc or Moon.

Here they will need some action. Aries is ruled by the planet Mars so the best solution for a fallen-apart Pisces with such a strong Asc is to get them OUT OF THE HOUSE. Talking about this won't wash. The Aries Asc will want ACTION (as opposed to Leo who wants CAMERA! ACTION!). Get their bodies moving, get them releasing some of that Aries energy. Get them to a Tai-chi class, take them to Judo, go running with them, try fencing. Any action-based sports. Not competitive as this combination is likely to bop you on the head if they don't get their way, and this book is written to help the Pisces helper......

Taurus Asc or Moon.

GET THE KETTLE ON. Get the cakes (low fat, sugar free) out of the cupboard. Listen for a few minutes, then get them booked-in for a holistic, healing, gentle aromatherapy massage. Sooner rather than later. Taurus wants basic needs met. On Abraham Maslow's Hierarchy of Needs, 'Biological, Physical Needs' is at the bottom and Taurus needs are those of food, sex, and skin. The BODY is important here. Once they re-connect with their physical self, the light will shine in their lives again.

Gemini Asc or Moon

GET THE KETTLE ON. Get the books out. Quote the Bible (either version, they're both good). Have the books to hand. Discuss. Discuss some more. Look at workable solutions. Listen. Nod your head every now and then. Smile. Look confident and that you know how they are feeling. If you have a handy vehicle a short 'trip out' somewhere will greatly improve their mental state. Gemini Pisces love to chat especially when driving or being driven. They will comment on passers-by, the weather, they might touch on how they really feel and in the confined space of the car will be honest about what's going on.

Cancer Asc or Moon

Oodles of sympathy is needed here. Cancer is a Water sign, and coupled with the Pisces Sun, makes the person who really needs EMPATHY. You can't just cluck and look interested here. Unless you have suffered what Cancer has, you're out of the game. Best strategy is to (again) get on the kettle, turn off your mobile, look calm and sympathetic, lean into the Cancer's space, mirror body language, and get the tissues handy. Cancers need to cry and will generally feel much better afterwards.

Leo Asc or Moon

The Second Fire sign of the Zodiac. You'd never guess it though because Leo thinks they are special and unique and need lots and lots of attention. 'There, there, there' works well. So does "How can I help, what can I DO?". The Fire signs like action, Aries likes physical action, while Leo likes company action. They want an audience to demonstrate and act out their story to. The more the merrier! You won't want tissues. Leo Pisces has to be really suffering to cry and they tend to do so in quiet, in private. Things you could 'do' would be to speak to the person's concerned.

Offer to back them up with any decisions they've made. Be on their side. Leo Pisces need confirmation that they are nice, so remind them of this and they'll soon be smiling again.

Virgo Asc or Moon
Now, I was tempted to say get the Doctor round as Virgo is so concerned with their health. When upset though, a Pisces/Virgo will fret, and fret and fret so you feel like screaming "CALM DOWN". This isn't a helpful strategy but does come to mind when you've heard every little detail of whatever was happening. But I'm not going to turn into Linda Goodman[17] and slag Virgo off, because they have that beautiful capacity to heal that no other star sign has so acutely. If only they'd see that, and instead of fretting about their own health, they could be healing themselves or others. Virgo/Pisces won't really want to talk, as talking makes them feel worse. They might take a flower essence so suggest Centaury, which is good or the Homeopathic remedy Ignatia. Emotional upsetments will also affect a Virgo/Pisces health and they'll get tummy troubles, or asthma or a whole host of seemingly unrelated physical conditions, when what they really need to do is lie down in the quiet and turn their brains off for a while.

Libra Asc or Moon
Here you might need the tissues again. You will also need calm, tranquil and pleasant surroundings. Libra/Pisces is very sensitive to their environment and as Libra is 'ruled' by Venus they respond better to beauty and no discord. They might need gentle questioning. Having tea is good but far better would be a big bunch of roses or a *gentle* aromatherapy massage. Things need to be balanced for Libra/Pisces and fair. Everyone has to take a share of what is going on. Point out that if they consider everyone else's point of view, they will only tire themselves even more, so it would be best to find just one strategy to 'move forward' with.

Scorpio Asc or Moon

Not much is going to be visible with this combination. Maybe only another water sign is really capable of understanding what a Scorpio/Pisces is going through. They feel things so deeply and intensely that if you were able to understand what they were feeling, you'd be a bit shocked. Dark colours, blood red, deep yearnings. The solution is to allow them plenty of space. Yards of it. Somewhere where they can brood and ponder and yearn without it sucking everything in their orbit in like a black-hole. In fact if you imagine black-holes you won't be far off what this combination is all about. If you're a strong person, stand within reach and be centered. If you're a bit fluffy, go shopping until they have recovered. There is not much you can do to 'help' as they will prefer to lose themselves in the emotion. They might write a song or a poem, get horribly drunk, or take large amounts of drugs. They might want revenge so be watchful of this and aware that if there are other people involved when a Scorpio/Pisces is worked-up, heads might roll. One useful tip is to get your Scorpio/Pisces to write a letter to the persons concerned, then ritualistically burn it. Doing radical things like this will help considerably.

Sagittarius Asc or Moon

All Fire signs want to 'do 'something when things go wrong. They want 'action'. The action that Sag wants is spiritual action. This combination want you to ask them what they think is the 'meaning' of what has happened. They don't want practical advice, save that for the Earth sign combinations and with Sag ruling our 'reason' for being here, try and get your Sagi Pisces to consider the wider implications of what has happened. You'll also score Brownie points if you suggest a long trip to somewhere Far Away from where they live.

Capricorn Asc or Moon

Now a Capi Pisces needs to hear the worst-case scenario, then work up from that. Get them to talk about what could be the worst thing that could happen in the present circumstances, then move upwards to the more positive suggestions. Capi Pisces prefer advice from people that are older than them. They feel better knowing that the future will be brighter than the present and they respect you if you are an 'authority' in what you do. You can't pull the wool over their eyes. Be formal in your presentation, don't sit too close. Don't offer to hug or comfort them (unless asked) and be realistic and practical in your advice.

Aquarius Asc or Moon

Most Aqu Pisces like something off-the-wall as a solution to a problem. They like things that are computer based like lap-tops or I-Pods so anything you have found on the Internet will interest them greatly. They don't generally dwell on problems and want to find a workable solution where everyone wins and they all 'stay friends'. In fact Friendship is a key word for Aqu Pisces, so suggest a nice day out with all their mates and they will immediately relax and start planning for it.

Pisces Asc or Moon

Breathe slowly and gently and listen very carefully when Double Pisces needs help. Even a small suggestion in the right direction will do wonders and the things to suggest are fairy-based, spiritual, past-life like, dream-based and not real. Take them on a past-life journey so they can understand what they did in a past-life. It will give them a better idea of how to cope today. Use gentle words, relaxing images, soft lights and candles. You can suggest white magic, chanting, Yoga, a retreat to a beautiful place with animals or birds, anything except practical solutions to the problem. They won't take your advice, so don't bother to give it. Just hold their hand long enough for them to feel connected to the earth again.

Chapter Eight

Survival Tactics

As we have discussed earlier, to truly survive a Pisces, you need to have your wits about you. They can easily stray into their world of fairies and mystical 'stuff' if you go on in unprepared.

If your Pisces is your child, it will be different to your boss, so I will describe how best to handle a Pisces in the various settings.

Your Pisces Child

Most Pisces don't really want to be born. They're quite happy, up in heaven with the Angels and the fluffy clouds, imagining beautiful colours and dreaming of white horses......so just being born can sometimes be a struggle. After a few years, they get the idea that they're going to be on the planet for a while, but the craving to stay in contact will still be there. Allow your Pisces child plenty of 'dream time'. Time alone with a favourite toy or book (not hours of TV, this rots little brains). Pisces children can like drawing and painting and sewing. Arts and Crafts will keep them happy for hours.

If your Pisces is a very watery Pisces, be gentle with them and imagine them as a tender flower bud. Keep them watered, and fed and cuddled. Watery Pisces need tactile contact, which they love.

An Airy Pisces will need conversation and answers and *reasons* for things. If Daddy goes away and never comes back explain why. I believe in telling children the truth, as nicely as possible. If Mummy and Daddy have got divorced, or Grandpa has died. Tell them, gently, what has occurred and it will stop their little brains from imagining the worst case scenario.

Earthy Pisces need structure and time-limits and places for

things. They are more 'things' orientated, especially with Taurus in the picture. 'My book', 'my Doggie', 'my blanket'. They need to know what is theirs and what is not. They need to know about meal-times and bed-times. The quickest way to stress an Earthy Pisces is to have an Air sign parent that dashes around doing millions of things, meeting people and "It's lunch-time" and no meal is prepared. Make meal-times safe and your Earth Pisces will love you forever.

A Fire Pisces need activity and some excitement. Not too much because Pisces always needs time to rest and recuperate. They enjoy the build-up to things. Knowing that they are going on a trip will keep a Fire Pisces happy for weeks. They need exercise (we all do but Fire Pisces the most) and some competition. Little Fire Pisces do well with oriental sports like Tai Chi, Martial Arts, Tae-Kwondo, and sports that involve stamina as well as energy. They like being with people, the more the merrier and generally, of all the Pisces have the most friends.

Your Pisces Boss

I've never had a Pisces boss but I've got friends that have. I suppose it depends what sort of work you're in but as a general rule, be clear about what *you* want. Pisces bosses, unless they have a lot of Aries in their chart, will generally leave you to your own devices. If you're clear and keep making clear by having meetings or verbally discussing things, how *you* do things, your Pisces boss will see that you're capable and trust you to carry out the tasks at hand.

However, if you have a Pisces boss who is emotionally all over the place, (something that happens throughout a Pisces life) then steer clear, *don't* get sucked into the Pisces whirlpool of muddle. Be consistent, alert but friendly. Don't do the work for your Pisces boss. They can easily slip into relying on you so much, they just turn up to work and expect you to do it all. Be firm but polite about what your work contract outlines are your tasks/duties and stick to them. Most Pisces bosses will keep their true selves rather hidden, so you might not even know your boss is a Pisces. Secrecy and fear of invasion runs through Pisces like a river, and they prefer to keep their true self under wraps, so don't ask prying questions. The two most secretive signs are Scorpio and Pisces and most staff will have no idea of their sign. But if one day you go into work, and the company has disappeared overnight, you can guarantee there was a Pisces at work somewhere along the line, and if they didn't enjoy their job, it would be no loss to them to not have it anymore anyway.

Your (male) Pisces lover

Now this is the one I get the most complaints about. Pisces men. Sigh. So where do we start? First of all, understand what sign *you* are.

If you're a Fire sign and your Pisces has got Fire in their chart, all well and good, if they haven't, then you're in for a hard time. Aries women will want their Pisces man to do this, and do that, and speak to so and so and organise this and remember that.............and don't forget the milk. Hmm. A Pisces man will put up with most of this, for a time, then one day you'll come downstairs and your Pisces man will have gone. He'll either physically go, out the house , bag in hand or he'll slip away from you slowly by getting ill, or drinking, or taking drugs or seeing someone else. Anything to avoid the direct onslaught of an Aries woman 'on his case'. This is where the Mars and Venus books come in handy 'cos a Pisces man, in fact *any* man needs to feel in control, and that's where you're going to have to agree to disagree. He's the boss, so are you. But he doesn't *want* to be the boss. He wants to mooch around being inspired, watching flowers grow, or reading quietly. If you're a Fire sign and you want to stay with a watery Pisces then please allow him TONS of space. Maybe even his own room in the house, that's sacred and HIS.

If you're Leo or Sag, being gentle also applies. Try to avoid cutting comments and 'advice' (I mentioned this earlier but I expect if you're a true Fire sign, you would have skipped that bit and just read this because you want to cut to the chase). He won't need your advice unless he asks for it. Your 'get up and go' is opposed to his relaxed attitude and that's the thing that gets to most of my Firey clients with Pisces lovers: the fact that he can be *so* relaxed when the boiler breaks or the car crashes. He's not you. You are. RELAX!

If you're an Air sign, again things aren't going to be too easy. This is called a challenging combination. I have a client who is a Pisces, his lover is a Gemini. She likes to talk, he likes to muse. They're both creative, artistic people but he came to see me because he was worn out by all that Air. All that needing to explain and rationalise and put-into-words. Air signs like reasons and discussions (I read that as arguments but I'm biased). Air signs want to verbalise things, chat about them, lock horns in debate......this poor Pisces was now drinking to escape the eternal nagging. That's how he saw it. He had no room to walk the dog, no space he could call his own. He was being crushed by a feeling of being dried-out like a bit of sea-weed left in the sun. Too much Air and a Pisces gets dried-up and cranky.

If you're a Libra there is some hope. Libran's like to be balanced and fair and there are similarities between you. Here is a Libran talking about an ex-Pisces.

"The main thing that I've found to be irritating about them is their slipperiness: they never seem to give a straight answer, and are hard to pin down to making any sort of commitment, responsibility or plan. The guy I was involved with even said to me once "we could have a kid, that would be great, just don't pin my feet down". He was a bit of a character really; extremely lucky, pretty, sensitive, romantic and charming, but also a rogue, a thief, a dreamer (a good thing generally, but too much of a good thing in this case!) and a social climber - he latches onto people who appear to be moving up in the world. He then

drops them when they are no longer of use to him and his schemes.

Come to think of it, the guy I was involved with had a thing about discipline too. I'm definitely not the most self disciplined person in the world, but he used to tell me that I was the most disciplined person he knew, and he admired me for it. Thought it was funny then, and seems even more funny now! My love affair was beautiful, passionate and intense - I'd never felt so treasured, and I've never felt that way again. I did however feel cheapened by it when I found out how much of a womanizer he was."

A Libran will want things to be fair, just and equal. A Pisces will want things to be beautiful, connected, flowing. A Gemini will want things to be interesting, snappy and cerebral and an Aquarius will just want things to be interesting. I once read an interesting summary of ideal places to take an Aquarian on a date.....an abattoir. Why? Because it would be **different**. Pisces man and Aquarius woman is another challenge. She wants lots of friends and to save the world, he wants lots of space and to go back to a past-life, or a previous dream.

If you're a Water sign, you don't need too much advice. You have a truer understanding of how a Pisces man will fare in love and war and you'll enjoy his touching appreciation of your love and care. Again though, don't try and make him into something he can't be.

Here's a Cancer talking about her Pisces ex-lover.

"I am just coming to terms with a major break-up from a Pisces, having also fallen out with a best friend of 20 years, also a Pisces.... I think Pisces people tend to be highly emotional and certainly indecisive. They are most passionate about how they feel and express that very well. They tend to be very intense (in my opinion) and give over their feelings very quickly. Only problem is they are always changing their mind, as if the two fish that swimming in opposite directions are constantly at odds with each other. This has had the effect of my being elevated to a very high place and then dropped which hurt a lot! I actually think water signs have the greatest capacity for love but also

because they are so deep can hurt in equally large measures. I think Pisces people are sensitive, kind, caring, loving and warm but can also when in a tight spot become over-dramatic and as cold as dare I say it? Cold as a fish!! Yes that about sums up my feelings, oh yes and they have their head stuck in the clouds, very dreamy and ethereal!"

If you're Cancer, he's not your Mum, if you're Scorpio *he isn't* having an affair and if you're another Pisces.................then good luck because as lovely as dating your own sign is, Pisces together rarely works out well. And I must tell you about my theory here. You date the star sign you have the most 'issues' with. Say your Mum was a Pisces, then dating a Pisces will allow you to work through the issues you had with Mum, in a detached way, but it's still your Mum and your stuff. My first love was a Pisces and years later I realised I was working through 'stuff' to do with myself. You get a sort of mirroring thing going on. All the things I loved so much in him, eventually drove me crazy. He wouldn't commit, though I found out (again, years later) that he had asked my Dad about marriage...................but by then I was already packing my bags as it was too late for me.

If you're an Earth sign your Pisces love has a much better chance of survival. Water rests nicely on a bed of earth, just be careful that things don't get boring. A Taurus male friend once joked to me that being with his watery Pisces woman made for a muddy mess. If you're a Taurus, your love can last provided it's exclusive. Taurus don't get jealous easily but they do like you to be there for them. If you're Capricorn you are in the driving seat and your Pisces love will stick with you, provided you stay true. Again watch out for the boredom factor. If you're Virgo you are the opposite sign to Pisces and I don't know any relationships where this has worked. It's not impossible but as Linda Goodman said fairy dust is what Pisces like and Virgos aren't too hot on fairy dust. Check out your Moon signs to make this work.

Your (female) Pisces lover

Once again, you must take into consideration what sign You are. If you're a Fire sign, your Pisces lover will seem beautiful beyond belief, mysterious, gentle, compassionate, she understands you *so* well and she looks deep into your eyes when you talk. If you're Aries, Leo or Sag those long, lingering looks might just be because she's off in a dream world and actually looking *through* you to a wonderful world beyond.

I had a client who was a Pisces and she was dating a Leo. They spent so much time mis-understanding each other and falling out. The whole thing was a struggle. He did have his Moon in Scorpio which sort of kept them together, but it wasn't a match made in heaven and I expect the karmic ripples are still reverberating somewhere in deepest Somerset.

If your relationship with a Pisces isn't doing it for you, then please pull the plug and allow them to float into someone else's life who will understand them more. If you must carry on, maybe because you have some watery planets, please give your Pisces some time to themselves: day-dreaming time.

What to do when your Pisces relationship has ended.

As Pisces can be such a complex sign, not here, not there, hard to define, hard to reason with, hard to understand, the best tactic is to centre yourself.

Pisces aren't famed for this ability.

I shall divide this section into the 4 Elements because that will allow you to ponder on the tactic that will suit you the best.

Fire Signs

If you're a Fire sign: Aries, Leo or Sagittarius and you are now in the aftermath of the Pisces relationship my best advice is to do the following.

Get a candle, any type will do but the best would be a small nightlight and light it and recite :

"I......(your name) do let you......(Pisces name) go, in freedom and with love so that I am free to attract my true soul-love."

Leave the candle in a safe place to burn down, at least an hours worth of burn time is good. Be careful not to leave the house and keep an eye on it.

Then over the next few days, gather-up any belongings that are your (now) ex-Pisces' and either leave them round your (ex) Pisces' house, or give them to charity.

If you have any photos, don't be in a big rush to tear them all up, as some Fire signs are prone to, then years later, when they feel better about the situation, regret not having any reminders of the (maybe few) nice times you had. When you have the strength, keep a few of the nicer photos, and discard the rest.

Earth Sign

If you are an Earth sign: Taurus, Virgo or Capricorn you will feel less inclined to do something drastic or outrageous (unless of course you have a Fire sign Moon...)

The end of your relationship should involve the Element of Earth and this is best tackled using some trusty crystals.

The best ones to use are the ones associated with your Sun sign and also with protection. The following crystals are considered protective but are also birth stones (p188-192 Cunningham's Encyclopedia of Crystal, Gem and Metal Magic, by Scott Cunningham)[3]

Taurus = Emerald

Virgo = Agate

Capricorn = Onyx

Take your Crystal and cleanse it in fresh running water. Wrap it in some tissue paper then take yourself on a walk into the country. When you find a suitable spot, dig a small hole and place the crystal in the ground. Think about how your relationship has ended. Remember the good times and the bad. Forgive yourself for any mistakes you think you may have made. Imagine a beautiful plant growing where you have buried the crystal and the plant blossoming and growing strong. This represents your new love that will be with you when the time is right.

Air Sign

If you are an Air sign: Gemini, Libra or Aquarius you might want to talk about what happened first before you succumb to end of play. Air signs need reasons and answers and can waste precious life-energy looking for answers. Forgive yourself first of all for the relationship ending. It's no-ones fault and time will heal the wounds. When you are having a better day and your thoughts are clear, get a piece of paper and write your (ex) Pisces a letter. This isn't a letter you are actually going to post, so you can be as honest as you want with your thoughts.

Write to them thus:

"Dear Pisces,

I know you will be happy now that you're in your new life but there are a few things I want you to know and understand that you ignored when we were together."

Then list the annoying habits, ideas, dreams, fantasies that your (ex) Pisces indulged in. Top of the list will be their inability to make a decision or be truthful and factual about how things are/were.

Make sure you write every little detail, down to the toothbrushes in the bathroom and the amount of times they said things like 'maybe' or ' I'm not sure'.

Keep writing until you can write no more, then end your letter with something similar to the following:

"Even though we went through hell together and never saw eye to eye I wish you well on your path" or some other positive comment.

Then take the letter somewhere windy, high, out of town maybe where you won't be disturbed.The top of a hill overlooking a beautiful view, on a pier during a blustery day maybe, on a cliff face, but do be sensible and don't put yourself in any personal danger.

Read through your letter again. Make sure it sounds right in your head then ceremoniously tear a small part of your letter into the smallest pieces possible and let those small pieces of paper be whisked away by the wind. I don't think its a good idea to dispose of *all* of your letter in this way, because a) it might be rather long and you'd be guilty of littering and b) you also run the risk of it blowing somewhere inconvenient, so save the rest of it.

When you get home, burn the rest of the letter safely in an ashtray and pop it in the rubbish or put it in the paper shredder and add to your paper recycling.

Water Sign

If you are a Water sign: Cancer, Scorpio or Pisces things will be a little harder for you to recover from. Not impossible but you might find it more difficult to extricate yourself from those sticky Pisces energies. You might lie awake at night wondering if you've done the right thing by finishing the relationship, or feeling deeply hurt that the relationship has ended. Don't fret. Things will get better but you need to be able to get through those first difficult weeks without bursting into tears all the time.

Your emotional healing needs to encompass the water element. So here are a few suggestions.

This is a powerful way to heal the emotional hurt that has resulted in this relationship ending. It allows you to use that part of you that is most 'in tune' with the issue. It involves your tears. The next time you feel weepy, collect your tears into a glass. This isn't as hard as it sounds. There you are, tears falling at a rapid rate, threatening to flood the world, all you need is *one* of those tears to fall into a glass of water. I recommend using a nice glass. Something pretty, that has some meaning to you.

Ensure the tear has fallen in, then top-up with enough water almost to the rim of the glass.

Place the glass on a table, maybe with a lit candle, maybe with a photo of you together, whatever feels right for you, then recite the following:

This loving relationship with you:............has ended.

I reach out across time and space to you,
My tears will wash away the hurt I feel.
I release you from my heart, mind and soul.
We part in peace.

Then slowly drink the water.

Spend the next few weeks talking about how you feel to someone who cares. If there isn't anyone who can fill the role, consider a counsellor or therapist. EFT www.emofree.com [8] is very useful in these situations and you'll find it's an easy technique you can learn at home.

Your (female) Pisces Friend

As with most of the advice I've been giving you, I hope one thing is now abundantly clear. It's not so much what to 'do' about the Pisces in your life, it also helps to self-reflect a little bit about who you are and what your needs are too. I could waffle on for hours about how Pisces can do this or that but what is most important to remember is who you are and what you want.

A Female Aquarius talking about Pisces

"I've always gotten on very well with people who are Pisceans. I find that they are always good to talk to about how you're feeling and have interesting comments to make. They can sometimes be too tender in social situations and small things might hurt them but if you don't make them completely hate you then there is always a chance that if you show them kindness they'll give you full love again. They are very open to other people's pain."

No Pisces really has the capacity to ruin your life, unless you want that to happen, but what are your expectations from this wibbly-wobbly person in your life?

One thing is sure. If you have a Pisces friend, remember they will reflect back to you a little of your 'self'. Their sense of personal boundaries are murky at least, maybe fluffy, maybe non-existent and they will change from one day to the next. Also think about if you have an Earth, Air, Water or Fire Pisces because they will all need different handling. And if you are Earthy yourself, don't expect your Airy Pisces to completely understand you.

But here are some gentle reminders and useful tips for checking to see how lasting your friendship can be.

First things first. Do you have any planets in Pisces? If you have your own Moon in Pisces, then you're in luck. Your friendship can last more upsetments, more disappointments, more hard times than any other combination. Your Moon will reflect back to your Pisces chum the things that are vitally important in this friendship.

And what is friendship? What do you look for in a friend? Someone who's there in the hard times? Someone whose shoulder you can cry on? Lean on? What about the good times though? What happens when those hard times are gone and life is better, will your friendship stand good times?

I've seen a number of friendships fall away when one of the friends starts to get their life together and their mate is still struggling for air. The friend who is having a good time, maybe a ball even, finds being with the (former) mate who is still unhappy, grumpy and resentful of life a challenge.

Don't be like that with your Pisces. Try and see some good in their life as being good.

Now the chances of your Pisces managing to get their life together is slimmer than say with a Capricorn, but it *can* happen. And when the chips are down, they will be there for you, listening attentively, being empathic, feeling what you're feeling............and when things improve, they will want to feel the joy that life has to offer.

If your friend is an Airy Pisces, conversations and discussion will be top of the agenda. Forums, chat rooms, telephone calls, debates, parties, creating 'something together'.

An Earthy Pisces will enjoy food, Nature, trekking, exploring, cooking and maybe digging in the garden.

A Firey Pisces will want to jump on a plane, deep-sea dive, organise a 'BIG EVENT', star on the telly or radio, been seen to be 'having fun'.

And a Watery Pisces will want to visit a Mind, Body Spirit event, feed the ducks or take in stray animals, nurture abandoned dogs, work with a charity to help 'those worse off'.

As you will note, there are different elements and different approaches to how your friendship will evolve. To keep the friendship lasting Do Not Spend Too Much Time Together.

The quickest way to lose a Pisces friend is to be in their pocket. They need space to reconfigure themselves otherwise they become a carbon copy of you. And that wouldn't be a friendship, that would be narcissism. Remember, they are a water sign, so your friendship will ebb and flow.

Your Pisces Mum

I must say that in the nature of the work I do, I don't get too many people phoning me up and booking an appointment to say they've got a lovely Pisces mother who cherishes them and makes them feel loved and content. So my experience of Pisces as a mother is unfortunately rather negative:

- The Pisces Mum who leaves the tea-towel on the cooker and it catches alight,
- The Pisces Mum who had violent boyfriends and was so busy coping with them, the kiddies suffered.
- Or the Pisces Mum who was ill, or bed-ridden, or died early, the list is long and sorrowful.

If *your* Mum is a Pisces, do give her a bit of a break. Gentle reminders that it's Monday and you need a lift to school, or No-you-don't-want-to-hear-about-your-Venus-in-Uranus-you-want-your-dinner...

Pisces Mums have been known to completely forget about the real practical world and things like Doctor's appointments, visits to the chiropractor, the fact that the shopping has to be done, the beds made and the house cleaned can be over-looked. These aren't things that Pisces Mums excel at.

It does obviously depend on what their mother was like. And if their Mum was also a Pisces (which is rare) , just accept that you will have to be self-sufficient and learn early how to cook, clean and keep house.

However, you're in luck if your Pisces Mum has got planets in Cancer, because that's the sign of nurturing and making –nice, scrummy-meals.

If your Pisces Mum has got a Libra Ascendant or Moon you will find she'll never be able to make her mind up about anything, so don't distract her when she has decided on something.

And also give thought to what sign you are. You should have a vague idea of how compatible you can be with your Mum, when you find out your own needs, but here a few tips on how to make living or knowing your Pisces Mum even easier.

First of all a Pisces Mum feels a deep soul-connection to her kiddies. Not in a practical way, but in a spiritual way. They will worry more about your spiritual path than whether or not there is food in the fridge. Not an ideal way of being but one they find hard to change. With a bit of practice you'll find things will improve.

I suggest the following to make living with a Pisces Mum easier.

Encourage them to build an altar. It can be anything from a special shelf in the dining room with lovely coloured crystal on, a few photos of you, a beautiful star-encrusted cup and the obligatory candle, to a fully fledged small table displaying 'special' things that Mum likes.

Make sure you delineate this as being the *only* place in the house that has the wacky-look because before you know it, you'll find coloured indian flags adorning the walls, fairy lights in the bathroom, candles on almost every surface in the house and your bedroom painted in fluffy pastel colours. Not good if you're an Aries. Explain that it will help your spiritual growth to have this *one special place* and your average Pisces Mum will get the idea and respond.

If you start finding empty bottles of wine or spirits in the recycling ask Mum what's troubling her, then ring a favourite Auntie (all Pisces have favourite Aunties) and explain that Mum is getting lost and leave it to her to sort it out. It's never your job to parent your Pisces Mum. They're quite capable once they feel spiritually in-tune again.

Spiritual retreats and workshops go down well, as do psychic/health fairs, mystical shops and magazines, candles, angel workshops, in fact anywhere where your Pisces Mum can forget about being a human-being for a while.

As a rough estimate, I'd say a Pisces needs to spend 70% of their time in the 'real world' and 30% tucked away with a fantasy book or alone with their thoughts. Pisces Mums get stressed if the emotional demands on their time are big, so try to reduce the amount of lost waifs and strays that your Pisces Mum might adopt, like stray cats or abandoned dogs or any being or animal that appears to be suffering.

Your Pisces Dad

A Pisces Dad is a rare, strange and peculiar being. On the one hand they can be practical, organised, good at sensing and knowing your needs, and on the other they can be (in extreme cases) a drunk, lost-case, addict or general down-and-out.

In all cases your Pisces Dad will want to parent you in the best way, so make the job easier by telling them what you like and what your needs are. Because Pisces (as a general rule) are so intuitive, we can make the mistake of assuming they automatically know what our needs and wants are.

'Dad just knew I wanted to join the cricket team' doesn't necessarily mean he will also know what you want to do about your life, your job or your car. Check back and find out their Asc, Sun and Moon signs and make a guess at the type of Pisces Dad you have.

Are they a Firey Dad, up at dawn, rushing off to greet the day, involved in multiple projects, enthusiastic about life?

Or are they an Airy Dad debating late into the night, wanting to discuss, read poetry, build castles in the air, bounce ideas around?

Or are they a slower, more practical Earthy Dad, fixing the car, digging the garden, lazing on a hot day, making fires on a cold day?

Or a Watery Dad telling you how they feel about things, or looking hurt when the present they have bought you tens of years ago ends up in the re-cycling box. Worrying about what they think someone thinks about you, fretting that you might not manage in the real world (that's a case of projection there), lending you money because they think it will 'solve the problem'.

Determine the element your Dad is operating under, then range your needs and desires so they can understand them better. For instance, a Watery Dad won't be concerned about your grades at school but will fret if you tell him someone doesn't like you.

A Watery Dad will want you to share things with him by hugging or close contact, so don't ask for money stood on the other side of the room, get near, hug, snuggle, then make your polite request. Taking into account that you'll be rumbled very easily if you're trying to pull a fast one, especially if they've got planets in Scorpio. It's almost as if they have an internal radar....

A Firey Dad needs to be doing things with you, climbing mountains, fishing, jogging, travelling into weird and wonderful foreign places. So if you have a problem or something to share with them, do it when you're both actively engaged in something, even if it's just washing-up.

An Earthy Pisces Dad will want you to voice the practical, down-to-earth aspects of your desires, something they can buy or teach or lend or give to you. They will respond when you lower your voice, move slowly and match your breathing with theirs.

An Airey Dad will discuss, chat, think, voice, sing even and will understand you better if you write down exactly what you want, bullet points, reminder notes, lovely long letters or phone calls. You could be standing on the other side of the room, but you do need to make eye contact and make what you're saying interesting and fluid.

Your Pisces sibling

Depending on how many other children are in your family and what elements they are will all determine how to get on with your Pisces brother or sister (the same applies to cousins and Uncles and Aunts).

All the usual Pisces rules apply. Don't drown them with your problems, don't boss them about. They might do what you want but they'll never forgive you and will make plans to get you back in another life-time. Check your own chart out and look for common ground. Do you have any planets in the same signs (you'll have the 3 outer planets Uranus, Pluto and Neptune quite near if the age range isn't too distant)? The major players of Sun, Moon and Ascendant are the ones that will, if understood, ensure the most family harmony.

Whatever sign you are, your Pisces sibling will at some point go through what most Pisces go through, which is a feeling of being mis-understood, not belonging on the planet, being away with the fairies and generally acting as if the world should look after them because they seem so incapable of looking after themselves. I strongly recommend the altar idea (see Pisces Mum) and if you have to share a room with a Pisces (say you're at college together, or on a school trip) be very clear about boundaries, where things end and begin because until Pisces are a little more grown, they tend to merge themselves with just about everything around them.

Your lip stick becomes theirs, your lovely picture of beautiful beings ends up on their wall....they didn't steal these things, they just 'borrowed' them but unless you make perfectly clear what is yours, and what is theirs, this will continue to happen.

As Pisces can be so changeable you might get a bit confused yourself if you spend too much time together. If you want to preserve your sanity (and you're an Air sign) spend limited amounts of time together and have different friends. Keep your social lives separate. Don't lend your friends, you might never get them back!

If you are a Cancer, provided you say sorry every now and then, you should remain devoted to each other through thick and thin. If you are Capricorn you won't get influenced by your Pisces sibling at all, and will find that in (much) later life you're still speaking.

The troublesome combinations are the signs that are called square to Pisces: Gemini, Virgo and Sagittarius. Accept the fact that you'll never see eye to eye but maintain a healthy distance and exchange Christmas and birthday cards and leave it at that. You'll never truly understand your Pisces sibling. Why waste effort trying? You'd be better off studying your own chart and looking for useful pointers.

If you're a Fire sign, make sure you have separate rooms. Insist on it. If you have to share keep your side of the room completely separate to your Pisces sibling. Pisces must have space to themselves otherwise they end up becoming the person they live with/near. I've seen Pisces talk , walk and act like their Firey siblings. They can totally lose their identity and become ill if they spend too much time with Fire signs, so if this is your element, do both of you the favour by keeping your personal space very, very separate.

If you're a Water sign you should get on quite well. I say should but with there being 3 major elements of the chart that we are taking into account, which mathematically means those 3 things can be in 12 different signs, making a combined total of 12 x 12 x 1 = 144 different combinations. If you were to take into account the 10 planets you can have in a chart, the combinations then increase to over 17,280.

For instance. You could be a lovely Scorpio with a Sag Moon and a Leo Ascendant. Your Pisces sibling has a Cancer Ascendant and a Taurus Moon. You are Water, Fire, Fire, they are Water, Water, Earth. You go fast, they go slow even though your Sun-signs are compatible and you're both Water signs.

You can see now, why Astrologers get headaches occasionally and also why the Sun sign columns don't really take everything that is in a chart into account. So to make sweeping statements like "Scorpios and Pisces get on really well" isn't entirely correct........well they do, in a way, but the above combination rather rules it out.

Of course, you might be an enlightened individual and love every person who comes into your social sphere, then the above advice will seem rather severe. But don't assume that because you are both water signs that you will immediately get on. Siblings and family members from my observations tend to clash most with the Ascendant signs. Our example above will find it hard to see eye to eye because one is viewing life through the specs of Leo's friendly, sociable and proud motivations and the other is conservative, quiet, withdrawn maybe and certainly very family orientated.

If you're an Earth sign, the above still applies. Check your own chart in comparison to your Pisces sibling. Make sure you have organised things to take into account your Earthy needs of security, steadiness, meal-times, nature and practical money-orientated specifics. Allow your Pisces sibling to connect. I don't expect there will be too much disharmony. You might even ignore each other most of the time! The trick is to check out your own Ascendant and Moon before you make judgements as to whether or not Auntie Mary thinks having a Pisces sibling is a good thing or not.

For further interesting information on this please see The Astrology of Family Dynamics by Erin Sullivan.[7]

I hope you have enjoyed learning a little about Astrology and a little about the Sun sign Pisces. I hope this helps you understand the last sign of the Zodiac a bit more. If you need more information please look in the reference section at the back.

I am writing this, while the Moon is in Gemini, in the upstairs room of a mystical shop in the centre of Bath, the hot spring city in South West England. I am a Pisces. I am happy in my job, with my husband, with my son and with my family. I know that all life is made from good and bad and I decided, not so long ago, to focus on the good. There is a candle burning by me and I know that this flame is stronger than all the discontentment in the world.

By the same token, sometimes understanding things is enough.

If we all understood each other a little more, then maybe we'd get on a bit better. I wish you all the peace in the world.......and happiness too.

References

1. Fortune-Telling By Astrology, The History and Practice of Divination by the Stars by Rodney Davies, 1988 , The Aquarian Press, part of Thorsons Publishing Group, Northamptonshire, England.

2. The Only Way to Learn Astrology, Volume 1, Basic Principles, by Marion D March & Joan Mc Evers. 1995, ACS Publications, San Diego, CA 92123, USA.

3. Cunningham's Encyclopedia of Crystal, Gem and Metal Magic, by Scott Cunningham, 2002, Llewellyn Publications, PO Box 64383, St Paul, MN, www.llewellyn.com

4. The Nature Companions Practical Skywatching, Robert Burnham, Alan Dyer, Robert A Garfinkle, Martin George, Jeff Kanipe, David H Levy, 2006, Fog City Press, CA, USA.

5. Crossing The Threshold, The Astrology of Dreaming, by Linda Reid, 1997, Arkana, Penguin Group, Middlesex, England.

6. Healing Your Family Patterns, *How to access the past to heal the present,* by David Furlong, 1997, Judy Piatkus Publishers Ltd, 5 Windmill Street, London W1P 1HF.

7. The Astrology of Family Dynamics by Erin Sullivan, 2001, Weiser Books, York Beach, ME, USA. www.weiserbooks.com

8. EFT: Emotional Freedom Technique www.emofree.com

9. The Instant Astrologer by Felix Lyle and Bryan Aspland, 1998, Judy Piatkus, London

10. 'Modern Text Book of Astrology' by Margaret E Hone, 1980, L N Fowler & Co Ltd, Romford, Essex

11. 'The Hidden Messages in Water' by Masaru Emoto, 2005, Simon & Schuster UK Ltd, London, WC2B 6AH www.simonsays.co.uk

12. 'The Twelve Healers and other remedies' by Dr Edward Bach, 1933 reproduced with permission from The Bach

Centre, Mount Vernon, Oxford www.bachcentre.com

13. The Astrological Neptune and the Quest for Redemption by Liz Greene, 1996, Samuel

14. Weiser Inc, York Beach, ME, USA.

15. The Art of Psychic Protection by Judy Hall, 1998, Findhorn Press, The Park, Findhorn Forres, IV36 0TZ Scotland

16. The Rules : Time Tested Secrets for Capturing the Heart of Mr Right by Ellen Fein and Sherrie Shneider, 1995. Thorsons, Harper Collins, London

17. Mars and Venus on a Date by John Gray, *5 Steps to Success in Love and Romance*, 2003, Vermilion, Random House, London

18. Linda Goodman's Sun Signs, by Linda Goodman, 1990, Bantam Books, London

19. Love Signs, by Linda Goodman, 1999, Pan Books, London

Further Information

Rudolph Steiner was the founder of Anthroposophy
Anthroposophy in the UK
http://www.anthroposophy.org.uk

Anthroposophy in the US
http://www.anthroposophy.org

Anthroposophy Worldwide
http://www.goetheanum.org

Astrological Association of Great Britain http://www.astrologicalassociation.com

Astrodienst , Zurich, Switzerland http://www.astro.com Great Website for accurate charts.

The Bach Centre www.bachcentre.com for information on Dr Edward Bach and his flower remedies

Index

BOOKS

O is a symbol of the world, of oneness and unity. In different cultures it also means the "eye," symbolizing knowledge and insight. We aim to publish books that are accessible, constructive and that challenge accepted opinion, both that of academia and the "moral majority."

Our books are available in all good English language bookstores worldwide. If you don't see the book on the shelves ask the bookstore to order it for you, quoting the ISBN number and title. Alternatively you can order online (all major online retail sites carry our titles) or contact the distributor in the relevant country, listed on the copyright page.

See our website **www.o-books.net** for a full list of over 500 titles, growing by 100 a year.

And tune in to myspiritradio.com for our book review radio show, hosted by June-Elleni Laine, where you can listen to the authors discussing their books.

MySpiritRadio